Pretty Smart

Lessons from our Miss Americas

*To Debbie —
You're not just pretty —
You're pretty smart !*

Penny Pearlman

authorHOUSE®

AuthorHouse™
1663 Liberty Drive, Suite 200
Bloomington, IN 47403
www.authorhouse.com
Phone: 1-800-839-8640

ISBN: 978-1-4389-3760-1 (sc)
ISBN: 978-1-4389-3761-8 (hc)

Printed in the United States of America
Bloomington, Indiana
This book is printed on acid-free paper.

Library of Congress Control Number: 2008911623

To my husband, Bob,
whose ever-present love and encouragement are my bedrock,
and my son, Justin,
whose presence in my life has always inspired me to be my very best

Contents

Our Miss Americas

*interviewed for *Pretty Smart*
No pageants were held in 1928–1932, 1934, 1950

	NAME	CITY, STATE
1921	Margaret Gorman	Washington, DC
1922	Mary Katherine Campbell	Columbus, OH
1923	Mary Katherine Campbell	Columbus, OH
1924	Ruth Malcomson	Philadelphia, PA
1925	Fay Lanphier	Oakland, CA
1926	Norma Smallwood	Tulsa, OK
1927	Lois Delander	Joliet, IL
1933	Marian Bergeron	West Haven, CT
1935	Henrietta Leaver	Pittsburgh, PA
1936	Rose Coyle	Philadelphia, PA
1937	Better Cooper	Bertrand Island, NJ
1938	Marilyn Meseke	Marion, OH
1939	Patricia Donnelly	Detroit, MI
1940	Frances Burke	Philadelphia, PA
1941	Rosemary LaPlanche	Los Angeles, CA
1942	Jo-Carroll Dennison	Tyler, TX
1943	**Jean Bartel***	**Los Angeles, CA**
1944	Venus Ramey	Washington, DC
1945	Bess Meyerson	New York, NY
1946	Marilyn Buferd	Los Angeles, CA
1947	Barbara Walker	Memphis, TN
1948	BeBe Shopp	Hopkins, MN
1949	Jacque Mercer	Litchfield, AZ
1951	Yolande Betbeze	Mobile, AL
1952	Colleen Hutchins	Salt Lake City, UT
1953	Neva Langley	Macon, GA
1954	Evelyn Ay	Ephrata, PA
1955	**Lee Meriwether***	**San Francisco, CA**
1956	Sharon Ritchie	Denver, CO
1957	Marian McKnight	Manning, SC

1958	**Marilyn Van Derbur***	**Denver, CO**
1959	**Mary Ann Mobley***	**Brandon, MS**
1960	**Lynda Mead***	**Natchez, MS**
1961	Nancy Fleming	Montague, MI
1962	Maria Fletcher	Asheville, NC
1963	Jacquelyn Mayer	Sandusky, OH
1964	**Donna Axum***	**Eldorado, AR**
1965	**Vonda Van Dyke***	**Phoenix, AZ**
1966	Deborah Bryant	Overland Park, KS
1967	Jane Jayroe	Laverne, OK
1968	Debra Barnes	Pittsburg, KS
1969	Judith Ford	Belvidere, IL
1970	Pamela Eldred	West Bloomfield, MI
1971	**Phyllis George***	**Denton, TX**
1972	Laurel Lee Schaefer	Bexley, OH
1973	Terry Meeuwsen	De Pere, WI
1974	**Rebecca King***	**Denver, CO**
1975	Shirley Cothran	Denton, TX
1976	**Tawny Godin***	**Saratoga Springs, NY**
1977	Dorothy Benham	Edina, MN
1978	Susan Perkins	Columbus, OH
1979	**Kylene Barker***	**Roanoke, VA**
1980	Cheryl Prewitt	Ackerman, MS
1981	**Susan Powell***	**Elk City, OK**
1982	Elizabeth Ward	Russellville, AR
1983	Debra Maffett	Anaheim, CA
1984	Vanessa Williams	Millwood, NY (9/17/83-7/23/84)
1984	Suzette Charles	Mays Landing, NJ (7/23/84-9/15/84)
1985	Sharlene Wells	Salt Lake City, UT
1986	Susan Akin	Meridian, MS
1987	Kellye Cash	Memphis, TN
1988	Kaye Lani Rae Rafko	Monroe, MI
1989	**Gretchen Carlson***	**Anoka, MN**
1990	Debbye Turner	Columbia, MO
1991	Marjorie Vincent	Oak Park, IL

1992	Carolyn Sapp	Honolulu, HI
1993	Leanza Cornett	Jacksonville, FL
1994	Kimberly Aiken	Columbia, SC
1995	**Heather Whitestone***	**Birmingham, AL**
1996	**Shawntel Smith***	**Muldrow, OK**
1997	**Tara Holland***	**Overland Park, KS**
1998	Kate Shindle	Evanston, IL
1999	**Nicole Johnson***	**Virginia Beach, VA**
2000	**Heather French***	**Maysville, KY**
2001	**Angela Perez Baraquio***	**Honolulu, HI**
2002	Katie Harman	Gresham, OR
2003	Erika Harold	Urbana, IL
2004	**Ericka Dunlap***	**Orlando, FL**
2005	**Deidre Downs***	**Birmingham, AL**
2006	**Jennifer Berry***	**Tulsa, OK**
2007	Lauren Nelson	Lawton, OK
2008	Kirsten Haglund	Farmington Hills, MI

List of Miss Americas from the Miss America website. You can find out more about the Miss America Organization and pageant participation at www.missamerica.org

Foreword

The first time I met Penny was when she interviewed me for this book. It wasn't long before the interview turned into a deeply felt conversation between two women. We discovered that we shared so much – a "can-do" philosophy about living and pursuing our dreams, passion for important causes, love for our children and family, and joy in all things handmade from the creative soul of individuals. Most of all, we believe that women can reinvent themselves at every stage of their lives. We laughed – and cried together.

My life has been a crazy quilt of experiences that have been exciting, exhausting, exasperating and exhilarating. Early on I learned to play classical piano and acted in school plays. Though I was a cheerleader, a class president in high school, honor student and Miss Denton High who wanted to make her parents proud, little did I know, as a small town girl from Denton, Texas, that a whole other world awaited me. I never guessed how much those experiences prepared me for my future. Here I am, all these years later, with memories enough to fill several books and hopes for the future to fuel the next several decades. All of it, from being Miss America, the first female pre-game football sportscaster on national television, First Lady of Kentucky, founder of the Kentucky Museum of Art and Craft and of Chicken by George, author of several books, advocate for Save the Children and the Alzheimer's Association, to a movie debut at fifty in *Meet the Parents*, has enriched my life and taught me the lessons exemplified in *Pretty Smart*.

Penny has also reinvented herself over the years. Out of college she was a high school art teacher. In her late twenties, she received her first master's degree in psychiatric art therapy and worked in the substance abuse treatment field, first as a clinician, then as executive director of a treatment program. Reinventing herself once again, she returned to school as a single parent in her mid-thirties to get her MBA from the internationally acclaimed Wharton School of Business of the University of Pennsylvania.

She told me that at first, with an arts background in a finance world, she felt like she was in a foreign country. But that didn't stop her from making her mark. After her graduation from Wharton she worked for an international consulting firm and held executive positions in the health care field. Eleven years out of graduate school she started her own management consulting practice. She has published articles and run workshops. Surviving a deadly form of lymphoma against all odds and dealing with the deaths of both of her parents only weeks apart, Penny never saw herself as a victim, always a survivor. Her son, who has his Ph.D. in political science, is her greatest treasure. Today she still paints as a way to nourish the right side of her brain. She inspires me!

When I asked Penny why she was writing about Miss Americas, she said, "I grew up watching the Miss America Pageant on television. When I thought about writing a book to motivate people to pursue their passion and looked for role models, Miss America popped into my head. All those years ago I must have internalized the lessons of discipline, intelligence, courage and grace you all exemplified. I realized that you've been part of my own inspiration."

Penny interviewed twenty-two of us and found that those of us she talked with have experienced the kind of challenges and joys that many people can identify with. She has such a warm way about her that I was comfortable being open about all sorts of facts and feelings. She even uncovered some interesting tidbits about my Miss America sisters that I didn't know!

Her research revealed that many of us are from small towns and loving families with limited resources who entered the Miss America program for the scholarships we could win at the local, state and national level. She learned that our backgrounds are diverse. We are the daughters of single parents or one of many siblings. We are women of varied ethnic makeup with strong faiths that sustain us. Many of us have experienced devastating tragedy in our lives and been confronted by physical and emotional challenges, from crippling childhood accidents, sexual abuse, the death of a child, a stroke at twenty-seven and deafness to Type 1 diabetes. We all have had to deal with people who didn't believe in our dreams and tried to hold us back. We've all known failure and defeat along the way. We've had to face obstacles and adversity. But that is just a part of who we are. As Penny discovered, those experiences only strengthened our steel.

Though our personalities range across the spectrum, Penny observed that we share a few characteristics down to our cores. She will tell you that the Miss Americas she met are not quitters, that "no", "never" and "can't" are not part of our vocabulary. We work hard to achieve what we desire and move beyond the boundaries of our comfort zones whether or not we reach our goals. We are willing to risk failure in order to succeed. Even if we lose, we never lose the lessons learned when something doesn't work out as we expected. We are passionate about giving back and making a difference in the lives of others. We share a quiet inner drive, strong roots and lofty aspirations.

Through her interviews with us, Penny learned that we all define success differently. Some of us have chosen to be in the public spotlight and, along with the others, to be role models for our families and communities. We've lived eclectic lives that have taught each of us important lessons. Always we feel the tremendous honor and privilege to be recognized as a Miss America and the responsibility carried with the title.

The older I get, the more important the legacy of being part of the Miss America family is to me. Miss America may be an eighty-seven-year-old institution, but in talking to people Penny discovered that the program is still relevant to so many people of all ages. Last year alone, the Miss America Organization awarded $45 million of in-kind scholarships. Young women can look to us as role models of intelligence, confidence, ambition and tenacity. We are businesswomen, actors, newscasters, teachers, activists, physicians, veterinarians and lawyers. As Penny says, we're not just pretty, but pretty smart! We never rest on our laurels. We always keep striving to be our best. I'm personally so proud to be part of this sisterhood of women who are trying to make the world a better place.

I've always believed that life is full of lessons, all worthy of being learned. I don't know what will happen next, but that's part of the joy and the challenge. For me the glass has always been half full, no matter what happens. That's just my nature. If you stay open to new ideas and fresh ways of pursuing what you want, anything is possible. You have to dream big dreams, use your passion to drive your actions, dare to be different and not worry about what other people think. It's a lesson I've had to learn over and over.

If you are ready to accept the challenge to take control of and responsibility for your future, this book will be of interest to you. Twenty-one of my Miss America sisters and I shared our thoughts with Penny about what it takes to be successful in our professional lives and our personal lives as well as the cumulative insights of our years. She has woven our stories into a rich tapestry of wisdom and inspiration. In *Pretty Smart: Lessons From Our Miss Americas* I hope you will find the encouragement and guidance you need to follow your heart all the way to your dreams.

Phyllis George
Miss America 1971

Making The Lessons Durable

Often we will read or hear something that sparks an idea, a thought, an aha! moment. We think, "I must do something about that. I can change my attitude, my behavior, my actions, my life!" And yet a week later, we're back to our old habits. I know. It's happened to me. It has taken me years to incorporate the lessons I have written about in *Pretty Smart* into my life. Even now, I must remind myself on a regular basis to pay attention. It does take daily decisions and effort to do what we promise ourselves we will do.

All the good ideas in the world are meaningless unless you put them into action. Most of the ideas in this book, at first glance, seem pretty simple, but that doesn't make them easy to accomplish. It will take effort on your part to make them real. If they were easy, we'd all be perfect by now.

You can make the lessons in *Pretty Smart* more durable by taking the following steps.

1. Get a notebook and keep it with this book until you finish it.
2. Draw a line down the center of several pages.
3. At the top of each page write IDEA on the left side and ACTION on the right side.
4. Take notes when an idea or story resonates with you. Write that idea on the left side of the page.
5. Now here's the revolutionary part: On the right side, write what action you will take to make that idea real in your life. It could be something small like getting up thirty minutes earlier to exercise, or something big like changing your job or going back to school.
6. When you finish the book, review all the action steps that you've written. By the time you turn the last page of *Pretty Smart*, you may have already implemented some. Celebrate.
7. For those still in the works, highlight the ideas that will have the most impact on making your life the way you want it to be. Pick the ones that are the easiest to do first. Plan your course of action and write it down.
8. Then, do it! Recognize that some of your actions or goals can

be done immediately, and others make take months or even years.

9. Keep track of your success. It will remind you of all you've achieved when you're feeling discouraged.

After you achieve some smaller goals, the bigger ones won't seem so daunting. And don't forget, persistence wins out over everything else, every time. Be bold and go for your dreams.

I'm interested in your voyage. Let me know how it goes. You can reach me through my website at www.pennypearlman.com. Here's to your success and joy in the journey.

Penny

Prologue

"Dare to be different. Be a pioneer. Be a leader. Be the kind of woman who in the face of adversity will continue to embrace life and walk fearlessly toward the challenge. Be a queen. Own your power and glory!" Oprah Winfrey

"Well *I* could have done that," has been the indignant cry of many people who recognized someone else's achievement. "And I'm smarter than they are!" is the pained add-on.

If being smart isn't enough to bring the world to your door, what is?

Being "pretty" smart helps...

The definition of pretty smart includes many additional qualities and attributes than just physical attractiveness and intelligence. Those who are smart and pretty have a vision about where they want to end up and the initiative to act to achieve it. They are disciplined about doing what it takes to reach their goals. Their passion, persistence and resilience push them past obstacles and help them deal with adversity. So who has been smart and pretty?

The women who have been crowned Miss America share all these qualities. They turn out to be not just pretty but pretty smart.

I met with twenty-two of them in their homes, at their offices or over lunch, in places like Memphis, Denver, Louisville, Los Angeles, Birmingham, Philadelphia, Santa Fe, St. Petersburg and New York. We would talk, then talk some more.

In person, they shatter the "it's only a beauty contest" perception with their intelligence, thoughtfulness, poise and eloquence. As Frank Deford, the award-winning *Sports Illustrated* writer and four-time Miss America judge, says in his book, *There She Is: The Life and Times of Miss America,* "No matter how many times it happens, the press finds itself surprised every time a beauty pageant winner is something other than a classic dumb blond."

The Pageant, started in 1921, has evolved from just a beauty contest into one that strives to provide opportunities for young women to stretch themselves in many directions. In 1945, Bess Meyerson was the first Miss America to receive a scholarship. As today's largest provider of scholarship assistance for young women in the world through both the national, state and local chapters – over $45 million of in-kind scholarships in 2008 – it requires that the contestants be competent, curvaceous and directed, even though others may disparage the role.

Many people don't see beyond the swimsuit competition. They think you can't be beautiful *and* smart. This complicated mix of beauty and brains has always been a contradiction in American society, which often dismisses the possibility of being both. It takes guts, creativity, endurance, lots of plain hard work and a fire in the belly to achieve that pinnacle of femaleness. In fact, contrary to popular opinion, the Miss America Organization had a liberal feminist agenda years before Betty Friedan wrote *The Feminine Mystique* in 1963. The Miss America Organization promoted higher education for women starting in the 1940s when women in aprons were more the norm than women in business suits. Tens of thousands of young women, who participated in the pageant system at the local, state and national level, have acquired the means to get a college education and have enhanced their skills.

Mostly small town girls with big hearts and big dreams, they saw the Pageant as an opportunity to actualize a larger vision for themselves. Being Miss America would provide them with a platform to achieve their dreams of a higher education, access to a broad audience to promote a social cause and exposure to people who could help them get where they wanted to go. Rarely was the crown an end in itself. And, as for smart, most of them were or became graduates of the finest colleges and universities in the United States, including Harvard, Stanford, Northwestern, Skidmore and Virginia Polytechnic University. Their ranks include magna cum laude graduates and Rhodes Scholar finalists. In 1974, a law student crowned a Ph.D. candidate. And then, they went on to make a difference.

They share similar qualities that propelled them into the spotlight. What came through loud and clear was the amount of resoluteness and dedication it took. These are focused and disciplined women with a compelling dream and a quiet drive.

The vast majority of them had to compete two or more times at the local and state level before they were able to move on to the national pageant. In the 1997 pageant only eleven of the fifty contestants won state titles on their first attempt. Many have competed in their state contests two, three, four or more times, and some have competed in the finals of more than one state. Once they got over their disappointment at being a runner-up or not even placing at all, they did not view the loss as a failure, but as a reason to improve their game. Their perseverance in the face of setbacks, and in many cases, even their own doubts, proved their mettle.

Others overcame obstacles such as profound deafness (Miss America 1995), a life-threatening illness (Miss America 1999) and a difficult and abusive childhood (Miss America 1958). They used the obstacles and barriers in their lives, not as reasons to embrace a victim's life, but to gain the strength and skills to achieve their heart's desire despite any perceived limitations. Many of them have gone on to champion the causes that were their platform, from diabetes awareness, school-to-work programs, veterans' rights and childhood cancer, to promote cultural diversity, obtain advanced degrees and become prominent in the arts, media, business, entertainment and politics. Most of the women who became Miss America went on to achieve professional and personal success and to make a difference in the world. They have become role models to their families and give back, without fanfare, in their communities. Regardless of what you may think of the Pageant, these women attempt to move through their lives with grace, beauty and fortitude.

Whatever your politics, events in the 2008 presidential race served to upset traditional perceptions of what beauty queens are capable of. The recent vice-presidential candidate and governor of Alaska, Sarah Palin, like many other women in politics and the media and entertainment worlds, practiced the skills necessary to achieve success through their participation in the Miss America and other pageant systems. Women like Oprah, Vanessa Williams, Diane Sawyer, Deborah Norville, Sharon Stone, Halle Berry and Debra Messing all wore titles in small and large pageants in and out of the Miss America system. In the political arena, Senators Elizabeth Dole and Lisa Murkowski, Congresswomen Shelley Moore, Marsha Blackburn and Michele Bachmann, and Jennifer

Granholm, the governor of Michigan, are pageant alumni in the Miss America system and other pageants as well. They serve as role models for all of us.

Pretty Smart: Lessons From Our Miss Americas extracts the lessons contained in the stories of Miss Americas from seven decades. They reveal philosophies, attitudes and actions that can serve as a model for all of us who have yearned to be more than we are. My life is richer because of them. I hope yours is too.

LESSON 1:
Beauty From The Inside Out

"It's wonderful to watch a pretty woman with character grow beautiful." Mignon McLaughlin, author and former editor of Vogue

People say that because these women are beautiful doors open for them. The former Miss Americas interviewed for this book admit to that. But what they will also tell you is that the door closes with a bang if there is no substance behind the beauty.

Shawntel Smith (1996) said, "I'm going to be honest and say that appearance does matter. Being attractive will get you through the door, but it won't help you keep a seat at the table, get the position, or have the opportunity. What counts is your intellect, your personality and the integrity with which you walk into a room. Your determination and perseverance are what will get you the job. A lot of beautiful women vie for the crown each year. So why not crown them all? There's only one girl who can win the title of Miss America. It takes more than just a pretty face."

Once you meet our Miss Americas, you can't help putting aside any notions about the women who become beauty queens. Though many of them are certainly drop-dead gorgeous, you can walk down the street and see any number of equally attractive women. It's not just their long legs or shiny hair that makes them beautiful. Their warmth, intelligence, poise and generous natures make them knockouts. The confidence and life-changing experience of succeeding at a high target they set for themselves and being spokeswomen for causes they support

1

changed their inner perceptions of themselves and can change our view of them as well.

Tawny Godin (1976) observed that people who may at first appear ordinary become more beautiful as you get to know them. "The way you carry yourself, the way you walk into a room has little to do with your physical beauty. You could be the mousiest person on the planet in terms of the way you look, but if you believe in yourself and know who you are, people get it."

As my friend's mom used to say, "You know, the girl who won Miss America wasn't that pretty before, but now that she's won, she's gotten much prettier."

From the inside out

Some people who are considered beautiful base much of their identity on their external appearance. You may be drawn to them initially, but if they aren't genuine, it won't be long before you are looking elsewhere for companionship. Unless they nurture what is inside, their external beauty will fade as they age. "Being physically beautiful can change many times in your life at any age based on your personality," says Ericka Dunlap (2004). "I've seen beautiful, exotic looking women who are arrogant, rude and pretentious. They would have been a lot lovelier if they had had a better attitude, because attitude determines your beauty."

Nicole Johnson (1999) will tell you, "Beauty is not make-up and curls and glitz but is found in struggle or challenge, the beauty from within." She recognizes that beauty can be an asset to open doors as long as it is more than physical. "Science proves that attractiveness is an asset in business. I would agree with that but I think attractiveness is subjective. I rely on attractiveness of the heart more than anything else. Along with my intelligence, my heart and my emotions are my calling cards."

Donna Axum (1964) agrees. "I think anyone who is attractive, whether or not she is Miss America, has a leg up on less attractive people. It's just common sense that it will get you through the door, but credentials have to follow. You have to be able to sell yourself, your abilities and your ideas if you are interviewing for a position. It's like we say in the selection process for Miss America, you've got to bring the whole package."

But many of the Formers discovered that their beauty and celebrity as Miss America could be a handicap in the professional world. It became, as Donna put it, a double-edged sword. "Many women will say that a certain person advanced so much farther because she is beautiful. That's an excuse. If you've got the ability and the professional fortitude, then jump in there and get going. Those are the attributes that people are looking for. Without that you're just another aging pretty face."

Our Miss Americas have the ability to change our opinion of them by their authenticity, their intelligence, their genuine interest in others and their ability to enlighten and educate without putting others down. They encompass charm, wit, warmth and wisdom rolled into one lovely package.

Too fat, too thin

You would think that these women, given the highest endorsement of beauty by winning the crown, would see themselves as others see them. Not so. They are just like a lot of us. Many of our Miss Americas struggled with their self-image when they were children. They say that they did not feel pretty and cite crooked teeth, big ears and plump bottoms.

Gretchen Carlson (1989), who now shops in the petite department, will tell you that she packed a few extra pounds when she was younger. "I was a tomboy, not into my looks at all. I struggled with my weight my whole life, especially as a child. I was a chubby kid who faced a tremendous amount of ridicule. When I overheard a guy I wanted to go out with say, 'She's a really nice girl, but she's too fat,' I got my act together and lost thirty pounds.

"The morning after I became Miss America I shared that story at my first press conference. I thought it would be inspirational to young girls to know that you don't have to fit into this perfect mold to end up becoming Miss America. I told the press that my brother used to call me nicknames like Blimpo. The next day the headline in the *National Enquirer* read 'Blimpo Wins Miss America Pageant.' That's how they spun it. I thought I was giving a positive message."

3

During her individual interview, Jennifer Berry (2006) was asked by one of the judges, "Do you think you're pretty?" "We were in the middle of a political debate," Jennifer said. "I couldn't believe he asked me that. I was not popular in school. I had big, thick glasses, crooked teeth and curly, frizzy hair. I've been 5' 8" since I was twelve years old and grew up being teased. I told the judges that I had never thought of myself as pretty because I was tormented and made fun of so much. I was just dorky. I'm twenty-three years old and I've been Miss America but sometimes I still feel like that awkward little girl."

Being with other women who are perceived as beautiful and accomplished can be intimidating. For many of the Formers, appearing at the national pageant was a bit daunting. Many did not feel that they fit the mold of a beauty queen, but they knew they had other qualities that would help them shine.

When Tawny Godin (1976) went to Atlantic City at nineteen years old, she looked around at the other contestants at a fancy dinner one night before the Pageant. "Miss Illinois was seated right where I could see her. She had a yellow dress on that night, long dark hair like me and false eyelashes. She looked perfect. I had never been that appearance-conscious as a teenager. When I became Miss New York State, the pageant people taught me how to use false eyelashes and made me cut my hair. I had hair so long that I could sit on it. That night I was looking around thinking, 'What am I going to do? I don't belong here.' I thought that you needed to know certain things and have a certain look in order to fit in. I definitely didn't have that look. That just wasn't who I was."

Tawny characterized herself as a preppy who wore corduroy pants and crew neck sweaters with turtlenecks. She knew little of the techniques the other contestants employed. "Some of these girls were putting masking tape on their butts to hold their bathing suits down and using contouring to enhance their bust line. I had never even thought about doing anything like that. I didn't even know that sort of thing existed. When I saw people putting Vaseline on their teeth I couldn't figure out what they were doing."

Lee Meriwether (1955) didn't know she had been entered in the Miss San Francisco pageant until the day of the audition. Back then, someone else could sign up a contestant. "One of the fraternities at the University of San Francisco where I was in school had entered my name. To this day I don't know who. I would never have entered on my own. All I knew about the Miss America Pageant was that it was a bathing beauty contest. I was not one to don a swimsuit very often. I grew up a skinny, awkward kid with big dumbo ears and a snaggle tooth. I was gawky and gangling. [Lee is almost 5' 9" tall.] When I didn't get a role, people would say I was too pretty. But when I looked in the mirror, I didn't see that. My first rejection happened when I was twelve years old. I was told that I was too pretty to play Mrs. Lincoln. It's happened over and over. I could have understood being told, 'You're a terrible actress,' but it has never played right for me that the emotional depth I can bring to the role is negated because they think I'm too pretty."

Several decades later Lee was surprised when she saw herself again in the 1966 *Batman* film in which she played Catwoman. "Just recently they had a retrospective of *Batman* at one of the theaters and they invited me. I thought that it would be fun to see my face on the big screen. When I saw myself I went, 'Wow! I looked pretty good.' Why didn't I see it back then? Why wasn't I aware of how I looked?"

As number eight in a family of ten children Angie Baraquio (2001) always thought her older sisters were prettier than her. "I always felt like I was too fat or too short or too something. When you participate in a pageant, people have this perception of you as being beautiful. It goes back to your own perception of yourself and your self-esteem. It took years for me to realize that the outside part will come when I just work on my inside."

Every one of us struggles with doubts about our appearance at some point in our lives. We worry that we are not pretty enough, tall, short or thin enough. We wish our hair were straight or curly, our bottom bigger or smaller. When we realize that beauty comes from the inside out, then we can nurture our nature as much as we attend to our appearance.

What the judges see

Many people misconstrue the intent of the Pageant, believing that it focuses predominantly on physical attractiveness. The job description for Miss America describes a broad range of skills and personality characteristics. As a scholarship program that promotes the ideal of a well-rounded woman, the Miss America Organization looks for someone who "represents the best of contemporary women… The youth of our nation must be able to find her as someone to whom they can relate; but, at the same time, she must present a professional image when called upon to meet with corporate communities…" She is charged by the Organization to "be able to motivate people from every age-range and socio-economic background to action and they must walk away feeling that having heard Miss America speak made a difference for them at that moment in time… She is on call twenty-four hours per day, seven days per week for the duration of her time as Miss America… The role of Miss America is only limited by the capabilities and the desires of the woman who wears the crown… Miss America must be able to push herself and the organization to live up to the responsibilities of being such a person." That's a daunting task for anyone, let alone a young woman between the ages of seventeen and twenty-four.

During the Pageant process, each of the contestants meets with the judges' panel for a twelve-minute interview. The public never sees these interviews, which are held during the week before the televised contest. The contestants know that their eloquence during this brief time can make or break their potential for being in the top fifteen and ultimately Miss America. They know that they must be articulate and knowledgeable about their platform, current affairs and a variety of other topics; be able to answer questions spontaneously and comfortably; exhibit an air of confidence and poise; and present their case as to why they should be crowned Miss America. That's a tall order for a twelve-minute interview.

Donna Axum (1964), who is currently on the board of directors of the Miss America Organization, lays out some of her specific criteria when judging. "The most important thing that Miss America does is talk to audiences, individuals and the national press and media. Her speaking skills have to be tops in my book. When I judge, I like to delve under the first question and see what kind of in-depth knowledge the contestants actually have on an issue. They've got to be smart. They've got to be quick-minded. On the other hand, they've got to be approachable, personable and relaxed when you talk to them, with a quick, easy wit. I look for a genuineness of heart and spirit, which is difficult to quantify, and a sense of compassion for people or causes. They've got to be talented because they may perform a lot on the road. I was one of the first performing Miss Americas. The more usable you are, the more appearances you have. They have to be stunning. When she walks into the room, people have to say, 'Yup, there's Miss America. She's the whole package.' "

The Miss America Organization used to define the qualities that Donna looks for in the winner as confidence and poise. Today the Organization calls it the "it" factor.

Tara Holland's (1997) goal was to have the judges see who she was on the inside. She felt that if she was able to communicate that, then she would win, regardless of the outcome of the competition. "The more involved I became in the system, the more sure I was that the only thing that would set me apart from the others would be how I conducted myself in that interview room. At the Miss Kansas pageant I had a very academic interview and was frustrated because I didn't feel that my personality came through. I did win Miss Kansas, but I was determined that the Miss America judges were going to find out who I really was. I came to realize that that there could have been another young woman named Tara, with long dark hair who sang opera and had literacy as a platform in that room. Somebody could look just like me on paper, but I was the only person who had the thoughts, convictions and passions that I had. That was all that mattered."

Tara ended her interview at the national Pageant feeling that she had succeeded in showing her best to the judges. "I'm passionate about the program because it promotes the complete package of what it takes to live a successful life. You've got to take care of yourself and your body. You need to work on what you're naturally gifted to do and know what your passions are. You need to be able to communicate well, then you need to be involved in your community in some way."

The judges I spoke with said that it wasn't the winners' physical beauty that set them apart, but their ability to command the stage, their charisma and self-confidence. The winners had that indefinable quality of poise that made them glow in a group of winners.

Vernon DeSear, a Pageant judge, watches the way a contestant connects with the audience. "The most important thing that I look for in any young woman is her ability to command the room and the stage." Leonard Horn, former CEO of the Miss America Organization and a judge, said, "There is a charisma, a self-confidence that comes through to those of us who are watching or judging them. You can see that positive self-esteem just in the way they interact with the crowd. On the stage you can look at all the contestants and certain ones stand out. They have a confidence about them. They know who they are. They know where they're going. They have a goal-oriented way about them. It just shows."

Rebecca King (1974), who has been a judge and is on the board of the Miss America Organization, describes the "it" factor. "I believe you could put a Miss America in a room with a hundred young women and you'd find her in about three minutes."

Having been a judge, Susan Powell (1981) is well versed in what that inner glow looks like. "It all happens in that private interview. There are strict guidelines about what you look for – about what Miss America should be. It's a scary thing as a judge. You will be changing some young woman's life. When she walks into the room and there is something about her, the way she walks, the way she speaks and the level of honesty with which she communicates, that inner something is apparent. It's a quality that is almost indefinable. There is no hiding under the lights of that interview. As a judge you immediately eliminate thirty-six people, just from those first sixty seconds. Twelve minutes is really long if you've eliminated someone in the first minute."

Four-time Miss America judge, Frank Deford, author of fifteen books including one about the Miss America Pageant. and an award-winning sports writer, came to understand what set the winner apart. "In the interview room you saw them differently than when they were on stage. If they didn't have anything to say you knew that within the first minute and half. You could sense it. I was always looking for someone who was smart and engaging and also looked good. I found the Miss Americas I met almost universally to be very attractive people. I remember the expression that was used – she lit up the room. There was just something about her. They seemed to be more in control. They didn't seem to be as programmed. That was a large part of it. You had the sense that they could go with the flow. They were prepared for anything." He confessed to a change of heart once he started to participate. "I didn't expect to like them so much."

Bruce Jenner, the 1976 decathalon Olympic gold medalist, who was a judge the year Shawntel Smith (1996) won, was impressed with the quality of the women who compete and the power of the Pageant to change lives. His initial skepticism morphed into admiration. "On television, you don't really get the opportunity to know the girls. But when you are there for a few days and you are with these young women, you get a chance to know them better. I remember how when I watched on television, I would pick my favorite, but the judges would pick another person. I came to see that it's because the judges know the person better. We see the contestants in different circumstances. When you're judging, you spend a lot of time with them. But when you watch you wonder why the judges picked her.

"My perceptions changed when I got to understand the quality of the women. That's what I would want my daughter to turn out to be – someone who is intelligent, who has great character, some talent and is motivated in what she is trying to do. I think any parent would be extremely proud of his daughter for going through that process."

Shawntel spoke with Bruce after she won. "He shared with me why he liked me. What he said meant a lot to me because the interview was the one area where I had been trying to set myself apart. When he saw how down-to-earth and practical I was and that I had a plan to promote my cause of school-to-work after I won the title, he knew I was going to be the next Miss America."

During the interview process that the public never sees, the true spirit of the individual contestants shines. It is the woman who exhibits confidence, intelligence and the belief that she has what it takes, who makes the judges do a double-take and put the crown on her head. She has that "it" factor.

Swimsuits and success

The swimsuit component of the Pageant has long been controversial. The Miss America Organization has kept it as part of the competition for many reasons. The first Pageant in 1921 was held in Atlantic City as a bathing beauty competition to spur local tourism after Labor Day.

Now, loaded with tradition, the swimsuit component is expected by viewers. In 1995 the Pageant surveyed the public about whether to drop swimsuit from the competition. Overwhelmingly the public voted to keep it as part of the program. Its entertainment value is not to be underestimated. Other pageants not affiliated with the Miss America system copy the swimsuit component and make it a centerpiece of their contests.

Over the decades its importance in the judging at Miss America has waned. Swimsuit now accounts for the smallest portion of the overall score and isn't as highly valued as the public might think. Both contestants and judges see it as another way to encourage young women to live active, healthy lifestyles and to be confident in any and all situations. The maintenance of a healthy and fit body is seen as a sign of internal discipline.

Heather Whitestone (1995) sees value in the swimsuit competition, though she didn't feel that way at first. "In the beginning I was aghast that I had to do swimsuit. I kept telling myself that it was only one minute in the competition. Today I think it's a good thing because the woman who wins needs to be in good health and strong enough to manage all the travel. If she can't take care of herself then she is not qualified for that tough job."

The swimsuit competition is a challenge for many of these young women. They have mixed feelings about having to appear confident and poised in not much more than a couple of handkerchiefs and high heels on stage in front of thousands of spectators and millions of television viewers.

Even though Angie Baraquio (2001) found the prospect of parading in front of thousands in a swimsuit daunting, she knew she had to play by the rules. She even asked her priest about the appropriateness of participation when her mother gave her a hard time about wearing a two-piece swimsuit in such a public arena. He told her that there was no moral issue. "Your mom is very strict," he said. "Don't worry – I'll get your back. I've got an in with the guy upstairs." Along with his support, Angie was able to take that walk with confidence. "I'm an athlete. I know I need to wear the uniform. If I want to play in the game, I need to abide by the rules. I told myself, if I could do that I could do anything."

She also counters the argument that being Miss America and especially the swimsuit competition belittle women. "If you say this is not an empowering thing for women, you're wrong. You can't knock it till you've tried it. The feminists say, 'You have to walk around in a swimsuit.' I said that I did it once, but I would never have to do it again. I just focused on trying to become the best that I could be. I was not starving myself. I was working out everyday, doing tae bo, lifting weights, watching my carbs and doing it the healthy way. I felt so much more confident once I did it."

Deidre Downs (2005) understands why the swimsuit component is important. "I had never won a swimsuit preliminary, so I obviously wasn't a standout in it but I think it has value. Your ability to walk across the stage in a swimsuit for twenty or thirty seconds and look confident and be poised is more important than if there is an inch of whatever on your thighs. The judges see that self-assurance and how you connect with the audience. Maybe you're scared to death inside to appear like that in front of thousands of people, but you don't show it on the outside. You go out there and be yourself."

As an athlete, Deidre was comfortable with her body and wearing revealing uniforms. But even she was initially taken aback when she first received the Pageant-sanctioned bikini for the first time. "You were able to choose your color but not the style. About a month before the Pageant it came in the mail in a little zipper baggie. The director of the Miss Alabama program was with me when I opened it. She said, 'I hope that's not the whole thing. Is that the bottom or the top?' I looked at her and said, 'No. This is the whole thing, right in this little baggie.' It was a string bikini and definitely more revealing than anything I had worn before. It was pretty controversial during the press interviews and garnered more media attention for the Pageant that year.

"The swimsuit competition is not a lightning rod for me even though I would characterize myself as a pretty left-to-center feminist," continued Deidre. "I was out there pioneering even as a little girl when I played in the boys' baseball league. I see it as more of the tradition of Miss America. Also, it's such a small part of the scoring."

Our Miss Americas discovered that they could handle anything when they were able to flash a smile, strut their stuff in a swimsuit and high heels and hold their head high.

First impressions count

We can't help categorizing people by what we learn about them at a first meeting. All of us make flash judgments. We decide at first glance who is dangerous and who is not, who to like or who to dislike, often with no conscious thought.

Like it or not, your appearance can affect your future. By appearance, I don't mean the face and figure that you were born with, but what you do with them. Someone once said that you never get a second chance to make a first impression. Anyone can change her appearance through the use of subtle make-up, a great haircut and good lighting. You can manage your body with regular exercise, healthy nutritional habits and clothing appropriate for your shape and size. Small differences in your physical appearance can create big difference in people's perception of you.

Kylene Barker (1979) feels that to be a winner in anything, grooming is extremely important. "I believe in first impressions. First impressions stick with people. My grandmother even at eighty-nine gets up every morning, puts on her make-up, has every hair in place, gets dressed and always looks beautiful." Kylene continued, "Beauty is first a positive attitude that you translate into make-up, clothing and fitness. We're living in a society today where too many people don't do anything to fix themselves up and don't take care of themselves. I believe in exercising and eating right. Taking care of yourself and fitting it into your life has to become a priority. Being your most attractive is what helps people be successful. If you feel pretty you give off pretty vibes."

"People don't understand what the Pageant does," said Tawny Godin (1976). "You take a young woman who wants scholarship money. Perhaps she's never felt that she was the prettiest or the best at anything. But once you enter the Pageant and you know that you are going to hit the stage, something happens to you. You know that you've got to be the best you can be. Sometimes it's more than you thought you were capable of.

"You find out that you can be a better pianist, or you pay more attention to your voice and learn to sing better, or you get interested in current events, or realize that a little bit of exercise makes a big difference. You are constantly raising your expectations and belief in what you can achieve. That's fantastic! How can that ever be a bad thing? The outcome has to be better than what you started with."

If you pay attention to your appearance, then people pay attention to you. Dress for self-respect. When you look great you promote your own self-worth. It's also a sign of respect to others. If you want to be perceived as professional, dress professionally. If you want to be thought of as an artist, dress in a more creative way. If you want to be looked at as a rebel, then don a rebel's clothes. Every cultural icon has a uniform.

The secret of perpetual curiosity

People who are curious about the world are more interesting to others. Sit beside someone who at first glance looks bland and engage them in a stimulating and lively conversation. Later you will wonder why you thought they weren't attractive.

Donna Axum (1964) said, "Those who have shallow interests or no interests at all other than how to preserve the skin that's hanging on their skeleton or the next shade of lipstick are self-absorbed. Women who are interested in the world become more interesting to be around."

The Pageant recognizes this truism by weighting the off-camera interview so heavily. Contestants know that they have to be well versed on many topics and clear about their positions on a variety issues. To prepare they read newspapers, study what is happening in the world and educate themselves about important historical events.

Everyone who ever achieved greatness was a lifelong learner. They never assumed they know it all. The people you associate with and the books you read will be the key activities that will change you the most. Spend your time with smart people and you will become smarter. Associate with people who are doing what you want to do and you will learn how to do it too. Hang out with big thinkers and you will begin to think big. Connect with creative types and you will learn to tap into your own creative juices. Besides you'll never know how useful something you learn today might be tomorrow.

Mary Ann Mobley (1959) said, "The day has been successful if I have learned a bit more about the world, other people and myself. I want to learn something new every day until the day I die. I see big challenges as opportunities for learning. I don't think about age. I feel like I can't wait to see what will happen next."

To perfect her craft, Lee Meriwether (1955) never stops studying. While she was in rehearsal for a show, a group of school children came to visit the theater. Her advice to aspiring actors in the group was simple. "Stick with it, study and never stop reading." One little girl asked Lee if she still studied. Her reply was heartfelt. "Every day," she said. "I read about the theater. I read autobiographies. I study people. I'm studying you right now. I'm watching how you are acting and reacting to me. Who knows, I may have to play a little girl or a woman who thinks she's a little girl."

Donna Axum (1964) believes in the importance of perpetual curiosity for herself as well as others. "I like to read, particularly biographies and historical novels. I've always had a desire to experience different cultures. I have an inquisitive mind. That is an important element of success as well."

If you have not focused on self-improvement as a regular part of your routine, you may want to consider starting with those ideas and actions that will have an immediate impact on improving your life. Understanding more about finances, interpersonal skills or technology could improve your debt picture, your relationships and your employment prospects.

Being a lifelong learner has greater benefits than broadening your horizons. Learning something new feeds your mind and spirit. Doing so makes happy new brain cells and will keep you younger longer. Research has shown that when you learn new skills, your brain builds new neural pathways. We spend way too much time feeding every part of our being but our intellect. We often stuff our thoughts with hours of channel surfing, our faces with food and dull our senses with drugs and alcohol. You can nourish your mind by learning to play a musical instrument, speak another language or cultivate your garden.

Why not put down the remote and use the time you spend flipping channels on yourself? The library and internet are great resources for accessing all kinds of information. Find a listing of free lectures in your area. Join a club focused on something that interests you. Go back to school to finish your education or get an advanced degree. It's never too late. In time you will be amazed at the confidence you've gained alongside new-found wisdom and skills.

Being perpetually curious will help when you don't know the answers. If you are curious you will be able to identify the resources you need and where to find the answers to your questions. Be patient with yourself. Learning takes an investment of time and energy that will pay you huge dividends.

Cultivate your character

If you want to attract people to you be kind, be genuine, be honorable. When you make people feel that they are important in your eyes and you show them respect, they will stand a little taller in your presence and remember you. Being nice doesn't mean that you let people walk all over you. When you show sincere interest in who they are, listen carefully to what they have to say, you have paid them the highest compliment.

General Colin Powell had a powerful impact on Heather French (2000). Since her platform was veterans' issues, she and General Powell were together a number of times at veterans' events. He told her about a Maya Angelou quote that she took very much to heart: "People will forget what you said, people will forget what you did, but people will never forget how you made them feel." Heather was inspired by Powell's words. "When you give people that attention as Miss America, it makes them feel special. It doesn't matter whether someone is two years old or in a wheelchair, every person deserves the best of who you are."

The responsibility Heather felt as a representative of all the Miss Americas that had come before her and all who would come after extended to everyone with whom she came in contact. "You realize that you can have such a profound influence on someone else's life. You remind yourself, 'Don't screw up.'"

Jennifer Berry (2006) saw how powerful being nice could be. "As Miss America I found that by being nice to people I was changing the perception that we're just pretty girls. Even better was when they would tell me that I was fun and smart and real. Creating the environment as Miss America so that when I walked out of a room people had a different perception of me was really cool. The way you present yourself – first impressions – is vitally important. The word beautiful is in the job description for Miss America. It implies so much more than physical beauty."

Our Miss Americas cultivate their characters and attempt to live lives worth emulating. Integrity and sincerity, intangible though they may be, are visible. Those women who become more beautiful with age exhibit such character traits in abundance. Integrity is evident in their interactions with others. What could be more appealing than someone who does what she says she will do, who takes responsibility for her actions and shows sincere interest in others?

Rebecca King (1974) said, "You have to have a strong moral compass. It keeps you focused. It helps you determine who you are and where you are going. You have to have that sense of integrity and character to carry you through confusing times. It's basic. You have to do what you say you're going to do. In business it can come down to a handshake. If I have an agreement with another attorney over the phone, it's done. People count on you. If you're not as good as your word, what good are you?"

We make emotional connections to people who exemplify high ideals. When we are with them, we feel the power of their focus and attention. They exude a genuine self-confidence. Just being in their presence makes us feel uplifted and special. That is how they capture our hearts and minds.

Susan Powell (1981) recognizes that inner beauty in others when she speaks of Jean Bartel, Miss America 1943, who successfully convinced the Miss America Organization to start awarding scholarships in 1945. "She was Miss America at a time when the Pageant was huge – queen of the universe. I just love Jean. I find how she is aging really fascinating. She's gorgeous. She speaks her mind in a forthright but gentle way. She makes me feel important every time I'm with her. I don't know how she does it."

When you make people feel better about themselves, they will feel better about you. We are drawn to people who enhance our own sense of self. Our Miss Americas know this.

As I witnessed their interactions with others, I found them to be uniformly gracious, warm and patient. A little girl came up to Heather French (2000) and Heather got down to the child's level to talk to her. For that moment, there was no one else in the room. Mary Ann Mobley (1959) took the time to ask a waiter about his family at a restaurant she frequents and write a thank you note to an airline employee who had helped her. Jennifer Berry (2006) and Shawntel Smith (1996) were welcoming to people who recognized them on the street. They all will pose for endless photographs with fans and listen to what someone has to say with patience and grace. These are the qualities that all great leaders and successful people have.

And when they see someone in distress, they feel compelled to reach out. Phyllis George (1971) has been deeply touched by the effect she has had on other people's lives. "We need to let people know that they're special. Sometimes you can say something to someone and not know the effect it has on them." She told me a story about a lunch she had with her friend, Sue Ann, one snowy day in Lexington, Kentucky. "Behind me were two women, one of whom was crying and couldn't stop. The other one was consoling her. As these two women were leaving, they walked by our table. I placed my hand on the arm of the one who had been crying and said, 'Whatever it is that you are upset about, it will get better. It will, so please don't think of the negative. Please think of the positive. I've been there. I've had those times. Just promise me that you'll try.'

"Not too long after, her friend walked into a shop and saw Sue Ann. She asked Sue Ann to tell me that the woman who had been crying that day at Southern's was planning to commit suicide. Her son had moved across the country and gotten into drugs. She blamed herself. She was recently divorced and was going to take drugs that very day. Because I had touched her and told her to not think about the negative things, but to think about the positive things in her life, she walked out the door and said, 'If Phyllis George can do that, I can do that too.' And she survived."

Phyllis, like so many of her Miss America sisters, believes that there is a responsibility that comes with the crown. "If we can reach out to people, we should. We've been blessed with this amazing honor of being a Miss America. By showing that I cared, I saved a life that day and didn't even know it." By turning on the power of nice we tap into the very best that we can be. When we lift ourselves, we lift others.

When Phyllis won the Miss America Pageant in 1971, the women's movement was in full flower. At that time feminists were vocal about their feelings that the Pageant was demeaning to women and would stage a protest at events when a Miss America was present. Phyllis tells of a time when she did an appearance at an automobile showroom in Dekalb, Illinois. Several women came to picket. "Here I am, a small town girl from Denton, Texas, at the highest moment of my life having won Miss America. It was a freezing cold day and they are outside picketing me. So I went outside and asked them to come in out of the cold. I asked them what their issue was. They believed that I was being exploited, but I said, 'This program gave me opportunities to get a scholarship and have a springboard. I got to play the piano in front of millions of people and now travel all over the country. What's wrong with that?' They said, 'You wore a swimsuit.'

"Then I said, 'You're doing what you're doing because it is important to you. This is the way you want to approach life. Well, this is the way this small town girl from Denton, Texas is doing it. I got a lot of scholarship money. I'm meeting a lot of important people that maybe can help me with my career. I don't feel like I'm being exploited. If I did, I wouldn't be here.'

"They said that I wasn't like the others. I tried to help them see that my Miss America sisters feel the same about the benefits of participating. I asked them to please respect the direction I'd chosen for my life." Phyllis may not have altered the stereotypes held by other feminists, but that group gained a whole different perspective on what the Pageant was really about.

Donna Axum (1964) knows that her celebrity does not set her apart or put her on a higher level than others. "Humility is an important characteristic of being Miss America. You have to be able to relate to people in all walks of life across the country, have compassion for their status or the problems that they are dealing with. If you don't have a degree of humility about you they won't open up to you. Humility, though obvious to others, is invisible to those who possess it." Now that's beautiful.

We aren't born blank slates. Each of us comes into this world with certain personality characteristics and capabilities. I'm not advocating you be someone so outside of who you are that you don't recognize yourself. What I am advocating is that you take a look at yourself and decide whether you are pursuing your potential. Each of us has a range of achievement within which we function. When you actualize your highest self you are at your most beautiful. Then you are beautiful from the inside out.

LESSON 2:
Make Success A Choice

"It's choice, not chance that determines your destiny." Jean Nidetch, founder of Weight Watchers

It's your choice.

You choose. Just like they did.

You choose your future by the very choices you make this minute, this hour, this day. You may have chosen to not do well in school, to continue to eat too much and exercise too little, to let other people tell you what you're capable of, to stay stuck in a dead-end job or relationship, to believe the world is against you. The list of reasons is endless. But so too are the possibilities to change all of that. You shape your destiny.

Daring to do more than dream – to strap on your wings and take the leap of faith toward your future – will ensure that opportunity, achievement, and personal growth meet you halfway.

It is simple to choose. You just have to decide to do it.

But it is not effortless.

Consistent effort and a signed contract with your dream are mandates. Wishing and yearning aren't enough, not until you make the choice, as Vonda Van Dyke (1965) says, to "give your dream legs." Once you turn thought into action, decision into determination and belief into movement then, and only then, will you be on a firm path to real achievement.

Some of you may feel entitled to success, to money, to fame, to power. Entitled means "given to." No one "gives" you anything. You have to work for it. You have to be prepared when opportunity shows up, ready to take on the challenge, as it surely will when you are open to possibility. You have to be willing to walk through your fear, find a way around obstacles, deal with adversity, deny the dream busters and believe in yourself.

If *you* don't, why should anybody else?

Take responsibility. Decide to. Then act. That's it.

The seeds of greatness

Shawntel Smith (1996) sat across from me in a coffee shop in Raleigh, North Carolina. "In some ways all of us former Miss Americas are completely different, but we all look at things positively. We're all ambitious women. We want more out of life. We're not ready to settle for what's average or the norm. We want to make something great of what we have in our hands," she said.

When she said that, Shawntel spoke for all of them. To a woman, the twenty-two former Miss Americas I interviewed believe that long-lasting, soul-satisfying success comes when they combine their natural gifts, their passion, their interests and fulfill their potential. They trust that they can accomplish what they set their minds to in spite of difficult circumstances and sometimes because of them. They understand that the seeds of greatness lie within themselves. Their belief in themselves is buoyant enough to carry them past their own negative self-talk, self-doubt and others' skepticism. They choose success.

They recognize that life is an extraordinary journey and that success is a moving target. Each stage of their lives brings a new perspective and new expectations.

"I've learned that success is based on positioning, always thinking forward to the next step," said a thoughtful Donna Axum (1964). "At every decade of your life you have to go through that process. I'm in my mid-sixties and I'm going through that process, probably in five-year increments now rather than ten-year increments. I look for things in this decade of my life that give me stimulation and joy and a sense of accomplishment."

They all had dreams from the time they were young and, through the decades, they dreamed new ones. At no point did they sit back and say, "I'm done." Though many found the highway to fulfillment often filled with boulders and potholes, these strong women persevered until they got to where they wanted to go. They persevere still. Each carries on the tradition of service and achievement that are hallmarks of the Miss America pageant. Here are some of their stories and how they made success a choice throughout their lives.

The grand dame – Jean Bartel, Miss America 1943

Jean entered the Miss America pageant to satisfy her burning hunger to appear on Broadway. She was notable during her reign for raising more money in war bonds than anyone else ever before. As the first college girl to win the crown, she encouraged the Miss America Organization to start awarding scholarships, which it did in 1945. She was the first Miss America to refuse to model swimsuits during her reign. Jean was always an independent woman.

The entertainment industry recognized her talent and professionalism at an early age. With an actor's equity card in her pocket as a precocious fourteen year old, she joined the Civic Light Opera of Los Angeles. The pageant then opened doors to a world she had been pursuing for several years. She took her exceptional voice and trademark smile around the world on tours to the Middle East, Europe, Canada, South American and every state of the Union except Maine. Ultimately, her Broadway dream became a reality when she became the first Miss America to star in a musical, "Of Thee I Sing." Through the next several decades she continued to appear on television, stage and in film, performing well into her seventies. Every year she still dons an evening gown, puts on her lipstick and heads to the Miss America pageant.

Jean was a single professional woman at a time when most women were homemakers. Her love for travel was sparked by her globe-trotting touring schedule when she was performing. She took that passion and started her own travel agency, Jean Bartel & Associates, which she ran well into her seventies. Jean didn't marry until twenty years after she was crowned. She met the man who would become her husband on one of her trips to Japan. Married for thirty-one years until he passed away in

2001, this grand dame, with her trusty dog Teddy, followed her dream all the way to the finish line and she is still going strong.

Age is just a number – Lee Meriwether, Miss America 1955

Lee has spent her entire professional life in the public eye. She is still acting, still learning, still stunning. Tall and slender, with swept-up silver hair, she still considers herself a student of her art. From small town dinner theaters to Hollywood sound stages, she has appeared in theater productions, movies, television shows, commercials, game shows, and soap operas. She has even starred on Broadway. "I've been working steadily for more years than I care to count," she says.

Some of her well-known roles include the first Catwoman in the original Batman movie in 1966, Betty Jones on *Barnaby Jones* for eight years, Ruth Martin on *All My Children* for eleven years, Lily Munster on *The Munsters Today*, and guest appearances on shows as diverse as *Mission Impossible* and *Star Trek* – she even has a sci-fi cult following. She has been nominated for a Golden Globe and an Emmy.

At forty-something, her spunk and flexibility were evident when she swung from a trapeze on *Circus of the Stars*. She performed in a twenty-one-city tour of *Nunsense* in her late sixties. Always open to new experiences, in 2008 she became the voice of Eva in the video game, *Metal Gear Solid 4: Guns of the Patriots*. Her intrepid spirit can in part be attributed to Meriwether Lewis, nineteenth-century explorer and later governor of the Louisiana Territory, with whom she shares some DNA.

Lee gives back in numerous ways through her involvement in several humanitarian endeavors and charities. She has served as Honorary Chairwoman of AbilityFirst, originally the Crippled Children's Society, and is permanent Chairwoman of their major annual benefit, "The World's Greatest Working Truck Show." Women in Show Business, a philanthropic organization that funds reconstructive surgery for needy children, has twice named Lee as their "Angel of the Year." She has also served as National Education Chairman of the American Cancer Society and as the Los Angeles Chairman for the Cystic Fibrosis Foundation. Lee has long been associated with animal rights groups and is deeply involved with Actors and Others for Animals. For so many organizations, she has been an angel. Her intrepid spirit is reflected in her two daughters, one of whom is a stunt woman, the other an actress. You go girl!

Substance, service and soul – Donna Axum, Miss America 1964

Throughout her life Donna has exhibited grace, resilience and a keen intelligence. Skinny and gangling as a girl, she had a powerful voice. She sang her way through childhood, then won the talent competition at the Miss America pageant. This southern belle disavowed ruffles and ribbons when she joined the Army ROTC in college and became a rifle markswoman. At nineteen she won the contest for Arkansas Forestry Queen. Her speech on *The Uses of Wood,* which she delivered two-hundred fifty times during the year she carried that title, so impressed her local congressman that he read it into the Congressional Record.

She kept moving forward through difficult times in her life and didn't use them as an excuse to not go after her dreams. Donna coped with a political scandal involving her second husband, then Speaker of the House of the Texas House of Representatives. As a struggling single mom, she put herself through school to get her master's degree, became a nationally recognized public speaker, emceed and sang at pageants and performed as guest artist with several symphonies. Donna has taken on many challenges since serving as Miss America. She has been a university instructor, author, civic leader, television executive producer and TV host. While teaching speech at Texas Tech University and Blinn College, she authored two books. For seven years in the 1970s and 1980s, Donna produced and hosted public affairs shows.

She has always followed her passion to make a difference in people's lives. In 1994, President Clinton appointed Donna to the President's Advisory Commission on the Arts for the John F. Kennedy Center for the Performing Arts. She is currently active on the board of seven non-profit organizations in the arts and education, including the Van Cliburn Foundation, the Fort Worth Symphony, the Arkansas Alumni Foundation and the Board of Directors of the Miss America Organization. At the state level, Donna is Chair of the Texas Cultural

Trust and is a founder of Texas Women for the Arts. Her strong faith is reflected in her service to the Southwestern Baptist Theological Seminary as an advisory board member, focusing on development and women's ministries. She and her husband between them have five children and ten grandchildren. Donna is a woman of intelligence, determination and vision, a force to be reckoned with.

No lesson is ever lost – Phyllis George, Miss America 1971

Phyllis has never been satisfied with the status quo. Her mantra has always been that if you lose, don't lose the lesson. She believes that you have to put yourself out there to gain higher ground. Throughout her life she has broken barriers and been a trailblazer. As a newly minted former Miss America, she appeared in numerous commercials and was tapped to be the first female co-host on *Candid Camera*. She became the first female pre-game football sportscaster on national television, showcasing her signature style on CBS's *NFL Today* for ten years. She co-hosted three Superbowls and six Rose Bowl parades. She later created two of her own prime-time shows on TNN, wrote five books, including two on the creative work of the hand, a cookbook and a self-help book, *Never Say Never: Ten lessons to turn You Can't into Yes I Can*. She is in demand as an award-winning motivational speaker.

When she served as Kentucky's First Lady during the 1980s, as the wife of Governor John Y. Brown, Phyllis took her boundless energy, restored the Governor's mansion and wrote a book about the process. She went on to found the Kentucky Museum of Art and Craft and support Kentucky craftspeople by selling their work through major retail outlets such as Bloomingdale's and Neiman Marcus. Looking for her next project she started her own prepared food company in her kitchen. Chicken by George revolutionized the fresh prepared food industry and proved wrong those who said it couldn't be done. It was so successful that Hormel Foods bought the company several years later. She has had a successful line of beauty products featured on a home shopping network. At fifty she made her movie debut in *Meet the Parents*. Phyllis never says no when a good cause calls. Through Save the Children, Phyllis has sponsored children in Appalachia since 1980 and now serves on the board of three non-profit organizations including the Miss America Organization.

Phyllis is listed in the *Leading Women Entrepreneurs of the World*, and the *50 Greatest Women in Radio & Television* by American Women in Radio & Television. "In the 1970s I was on the cover of *People* magazine as the 'First Lady of the Locker Room.' In the 1980s, I was again on the cover of *People* as the 'First Lady of Kentucky.' In the 1990s my best one yet: *Poultry Processing* magazine put me on their cover as the 'First Lady of Chicken.' Now I can die a happy woman!" But she's not done yet. She was awarded the prestigious Rita Hayworth award for her work as an advocate and spokeswoman for the Alzheimer's Association, a task she took on after her mother and best friend passed away from the disease. Phyllis's most difficult role ever was as her mother's primary long-distance caregiver for ten years. She is now writing a book on caregiving to help others dealing with this heartbreaking disease. When she talks about her television reporter daughter and her entrepreneur son, Phyllis glows with pride. The word "never" is not in this woman's vocabulary.

Her own woman – Rebecca King, Miss America 1974

Rebecca, who had grown up in a small Colorado farming community, saw the Miss America pageant system as a way to fund her way through law school. It did that and more. The judges recognized Rebecca as a herald of the new feminism. At the Miss America Pageant's morning-after breakfast following her crowning, Rebecca shared her feminist political views to the consternation of some and the applause of others. Up until and including her crowning, the interview section of the competition carried little formal weight in the judging. As a representative of the thinking modern American woman, she convinced the Miss America Organization to create a separate category with its own points for the interview segment.

She used her scholarship money to complete her law degree at University of Denver Law School. Before she started her own law practice, she was Director of Marketing, Community and Public Relations for the Colorado Regional Transportation District. Since then she has had her own legal practice specializing in civil litigation and family law.

Helping kids see the possibilities in life is one of her passions. Rebecca works with children's organizations and has produced and directed several plays, musicals and theatrical performances. She hosts school groups at the judicial buildings in Denver. Audiences of young women at many schools and organizations have been empowered by her message of limitless possibilities. Actively sought after for career development days at regional schools, she inspires teenagers to find direction in their lives and raise the bar of their expectations.

Despite her busy schedule, Rebecca says yes when a worthy cause asks. Like so many other Miss Americas, community service is always on her to-do list. She has served in numerous leadership roles for a variety of charitable organizations including the Colorado Women's College, Mercy Housing Southeast Community, Volunteers of America, serves on the board of the Miss America Organization and has been the national spokesperson for the Business and Professional Women's Foundation. She is married to a sculptor and has two children. Rebecca showed leadership qualities from childhood on. It's what she knows how to do.

Diminutive powerhouse – Gretchen Carlson, Miss America 1989

Gretchen's blond hair, blue eyes and petite stature belie a woman of perseverance and courage. As a child she was an award-winning classical violin prodigy and played and studied at the prestigious Aspen Music Festival for several summers. She was one of its youngest student performers. Graduating with honors from Stanford University with a self-designed major in organizational behavior, she later studied at Oxford University in England.

When winning the crown opened new worlds to her, she decided to change direction and pursue a career in television news reporting. Willing to pay her dues, she started at the bottom as a rookie political reporter at an ABC affiliate in Richmond, Virginia. Over the next decade she moved on to Cincinnati, Cleveland and Dallas, where she became an anchor. In 2000, CBS News in New York called and Gretchen ended up hosting *The Early Show*. While at CBS, she covered breaking news events, both nationally and internationally, including the

Columbia space shuttle disaster, the capture of the Washington D.C. sniper, the World Trade Center attack on September 11th and the G-8 Summit in Genoa, Italy.

These days you can find Gretchen as co-host of Fox News Channel's national morning news show, "Fox and Friends." Her work has been honored with three American Women in Radio and Television National Awards (Gracie Awards), including Best Network Feature.

Family tradition taught her that service to others is an obligation in life. Gretchen gives back to causes she believes in. She is a national celebrity spokesperson for the March of Dimes and continues to be an advocate of the arts. Along the way, she married and had two children. This diminutive powerhouse who shops in the petite department lights up the television screen every morning with wit, insightful commentary and charm.

Woman with a cause – Nicole Johnson, Miss America 1999

Nicole copes with Type I diabetes with grace and fortitude. She has taken a challenge in her life and turned it to good. With two master's degrees posted on her wall, and four authored books in her tote, Nicole is an ardent advocate for diabetes prevention, education, awareness and research, traveling and speaking both nationally and internationally.

Her passion has pushed her to the forefront of diabetes advocacy. Nicole has lobbied the U.S. Congress. In partnership with the American Diabetes Association, she has helped to pass insurance legislation on the state level providing improved access to care for people with diabetes. Over the last several years, she has helped generate more than $16 million to support diabetes research and development.

Even the U.S. Defense Department has turned to Nicole for assistance with related diabetes legislation, appropriations requests and product development. She has participated in strategic planning for various Departments of Health on the state and federal levels. Working with major pharmaceutical companies, she helps to create diabetes awareness programs for patients and the general public. As if that isn't enough, she co-hosts dLife TV, a weekly Emmy award-winning diabetes education television program on CNBC.

Nicole has received numerous national and international awards for her important work in diabetes education from such organizations as the American Diabetes Association, the American Association of Clinical Endocrinologists, the Japan Association for Diabetes Care and Education, and the Polish Diabetes Association.

And, she is the mother of an active three-year-old. This woman, just a decade from her crowning, has made a positive impact in the lives of thousands of individuals and families affected by diabetes. Meeting her for the first time, I was struck by the light emanating from within her.

None of these women sat around waiting for something to happen. These fabulous Miss Americas are rebellious women. They rebel against others' cramped vision of what is possible. They rebel against their own limiting beliefs. They rebel against constraints and narrow minds. They forge their own path. It *is* what's inside that counts. They choose success.

Victory is what you make it

Success isn't static, nor is it a single end point. Once you win the crown, then what? Once the excitement of moving into the corner office wears off, what's next on your agenda? Paying off the mortgage, winning a marathon, getting your master's degree are only the stepping-stones to the next phase of your life. It's just human nature to rest on your laurels for a brief moment of glory and then peer around the corner to see what's next.

Though success is often described as a "thing to have" (wealth) or "state to be" (wealthy) it is much more about a state of being and how we feel. We have targets that often move as we get closer to them. That last five pounds is as elusive as ever. Whatever is in the bank account is never enough, although there was a time when that number seemed as if it would last forever. Obtaining a degree just means that that there is more to learn. That coveted job still requires ongoing excellence. So we continue to strive. Viewing success as a process just seems to make more sense.

Rebecca King (1974) thinks that too many people have as a primary definition of success the acquisition of wealth. "I don't define my personal success by dollars and cents. I find success when I feel an emotional fulfillment, whether it is in a project that is successful or something else. I have that inner sense of satisfaction. I don't need a pat on the back. There's this internal mechanism that tells me I have arrived."

Following your dreams is a journey of discovery because the very journey changes us. We learn. We are challenged. We grow.

When I interviewed the Formers (as former Miss Americas refer to themselves), the first question I asked them was how they defined success for themselves. It turns out that they all have similar feelings, whether they were crowned Miss America in 1956 or 2006. Listen to some of their voices.

Shawntel Smith (1996) said, "Success is made up of the physical, spiritual, mental and emotional. To have true success for oneself is not about an accolade. It's not about a crown. It's truly about being happy with your whole person.

"For your career," continued Shawntel, "you have professional goals in front of you that you are striving to achieve. We are all creatures of accomplishment and we want to make an impact in whatever we're doing. There has to be a satisfaction in the doing of what you are doing. If you have that goal in front of you – whether it's to be Miss America, or to attain a doctoral degree, or become the CEO of your own company, or invent something that hasn't been thought of before – all that we strive to achieve – if we're able one day to make all of those stars align, that to me is the ultimate success."

Phyllis George (1971) spoke passionately. "A visionary can see what is out there, and, more important, what is not out there. That's how you find a void and fill it. It takes someone with a creative spirit and a creative mind to see what is missing. When you zero in on your own unique talent or idea and it's something no one else is doing, you've found your niche."

People who feel successful throughout their lives do that which is meaningful to them. For them, the final result is important, but the satisfaction comes from creating a life they want and being a positive force in the lives of others along the way.

For Heather French (2000) the most satisfying form of success comes from making a difference. "Too many young women don't know what true success is because they look at the superficial - what Hollywood teaches them and what the media says. We all need to have goals that we set for ourselves. Each one of us is accountable for defining our purpose. Because my father was in the Vietnam War and struggled for years after, helping veterans became my cause.

"Miss America showed me that so many things are possible. So many people are shortsighted about what possibilities exist. Even though my family was financially challenged and had to overcome a lot, my parents taught me that anything is possible. Only you say you can't."

Marilyn Van Derbur (1958), herself a victim of incest, is passionate about helping other victims of sexual abuse. "I love the George Bernard Shaw quote 'I want to be thoroughly used up when I die.' I feel successful because I found my passion. It is extremely demanding, emotionally and physically. I am filling a niche that is uniquely mine. In many instances, I'm the only one who can help this particular person, in this particular way, at this particular time. That is a privilege and a gift and an enormous responsibility."

They all believe that as long as they gave their very best, they succeeded.

Jennifer Berry (2006), newly minted from her year of service as Miss America, offered this. "Success is knowing deep in my heart that I gave one hundred percent, whether I succeeded in reaching that goal or not…no matter how many times I failed. Throughout my five years of competing, even though I walked off the stage without the crown four years in a row, I always wanted to walk away saying, 'I succeeded that year. I gave it all I had.'"

Angie Baraquio (2001) took strength from her Hawaiian heritage. "I used to think that success is whenever you are happy at the end of the day with what you've accomplished. Now, today, as a mom, as a wife, as a professional, it's not just about the accomplishments. It's not just about the money you make. It's about the impact that you've made with your life. It's a struggle, honestly, every day.

"Today, the deeper meaning is the harmony, beauty and balance inherent in hula that I've created in my life. The financial rewards come when you are in harmony. Everything comes when you're in balance and true to who you are. So I'm always striving to find that harmony and that balance and that to me is success."

Vonda Van Dyke (1965) always followed her own path. "Success is a very individual thing. For me, it's being the best I can be. I can't compare myself to somebody else. I have a different background, different talent, different view on things. If I'm happy with the way I'm thinking and with what I'm doing, that's what makes me a success. I don't feel like I'm measured by other people. I probably am, but I just don't pay attention to that. My success is within me."

Success doesn't just appear. They all recognize the hard work and planning that getting to their goal requires.

"I wasn't born with a silver spoon in my mouth," said Kylene Barker (1979), who jumped into her post-Miss America career as a women's clothing store owner without looking back. "Anything that I wanted to achieve, whether it was featured twirler at my high school or cheerleading captain, to riding bareback on my horse Blaze while I was growing up, and later opening my own clothing store, took practice and lots of focused effort. Being successful means setting a goal, planning a strategy, assessing your assets and liabilities, what you're strong in, what you're not so strong in and doing the hard work. You have to take risks to achieve success."

With maturity comes a changing definition of what being successful means.

Ericka Dunlap (2004) shared her perspective with me. "My view of success has changed a lot over the years. I don't consider status and money as much as I did before. I think it is so very important to look for success beyond the fame and the fortune, to be able to say you did it and you overcame it. It's a personal testament of your struggle and your triumph.

"It's really an opportunity for other people to be inspired by what you did. In this country there is a culture that says you must make money and money will make you happy, which it doesn't. With maturity you understand more and more that money cannot buy any of the essential qualities that you need to be a decent human being. It cannot buy you class. It cannot buy you integrity."

33

A woman of elegance and grace, Lynda Mead (1960) started her own interior design business in her forties. "If you're not successful in your relationships with the people you love, then you're not successful, no matter how much success you may have professionally. Being able to impact people's lives positively is really the definition of success. When I was twenty I probably wouldn't have answered that question that way. Success would be having a big career, making a lot of money and that sort of thing. Of course, you don't know anything when you're twenty."

These former Miss Americas, champions every one, found that the challenges they confronted, the people who crossed their paths and the events that tested them during their year of traveling around the country for the Miss America Organization, changed their perspective. Small town girls were suddenly exposed to big city lights and mean streets, corporate executives, people in need, and the halls of Congress. Big town girls found themselves on a national and international stage, sometimes overwhelmed by the responsibility of having earned the crown. They all had to grow up at warp speed. With those new experiences came fresh insights into what was important to them.

Tara Holland (1997) shared her thoughts. "My goals have always been long-sighted. That's one of the things that people miss. For so many, their dreams are 'all I want is to be Miss Nashville.' So if that's all you want, that's all you're going to get.

"My goal was to be Miss America. When I first began competing at seventeen I was drawn to the glamour and glitz of the crown. But as I got into the program, and I realized the voice that comes with it, my passion changed. I saw how I now had the opportunity to use that voice to impact other people. Even when I had just a local title, I saw the impact it had on little girls and people of all ages. It gave me an opportunity to speak something into their lives that would hopefully have a positive impact on them."

The world does not define success. You define success. When the door closes at night, the only person you have to answer to is yourself. So don't ask the world. Ask your heart.

No magic bullets

Many people keep looking for that secret, elusive and mysterious, that will tell them which lottery ticket for life to buy. They are perplexed by what others seem to achieve so effortlessly. Regardless of their talents and abilities, these underachievers are unable to start the ignition of their ambition. They don't recognize the years of perseverance, discipline and stick-to-it-iveness that it takes to become an overnight success.

How smart you are isn't really the measure of whether or not you will be successful. Often really bright people become complacent and coast on their natural gifts, rather than recognizing the context of that gift and maximizing its effect.

People who succeed hold to a vision and a purpose. They live their lives making decisions that are measured against whether those decisions will move them toward their vision. They know that it is the daily choices they make that mean the difference between failure and success. The women who became Miss America succeed because they define their purpose and make it a habit to check that their everyday actions support the achievement of their goal. They create the life they want.

When you enrich your life and the lives of others you are a success. When you complete a task and achieve a goal, you are successful. The goal may be small, like organizing your closet or exercising three times a week, or big, like starting a company or going to graduate school. And when the ultimate goal is out of reach, as long as you've given it your best, that's success too.

Fulfilling a dream is a choice you can make. It doesn't happen by chance. If you want life to take a direction that you are in control of, only you can decide to choose success and accept the challenge to be proactive in pursuit of your goal. That, my Miss America, is up to you. You have to have the burning hots for your dream. If you do, then your passion will push you to do whatever it takes to get where you want to go. People who follow their passion don't experience burnout. The journey energizes them.

Dream your dream, do what you must to give it legs, and believe in your success. It's all you deserve. What are you waiting for?

LESSON 3:
You've Got What It Takes

"People begin to become successful the minute they decide to be." Harvey Mackay, nationally syndicated columnist and businessman

You might think that the women who become Miss America aren't like us mere mortals, blessed as they are with beauty, brains and opportunity, but that's not true. The attributes that helped them triumph over the other contestants had little to do with their looks. After all, they were only one out of a large group of equally beautiful women.

Some hard-to-define quality set them apart from the other contestants. These women won that glittering crown and found later success by employing the same traits that are accessible to all of us. Their intelligence and belief in their capabilities along with discipline and perseverance created an aura of poise and maturity that the judges saw... and felt. These women weren't just starry-eyed about their future. They took action and didn't let anything stop them. Each of them exhibits the characteristics of successful people.

Although each of us has a varied mix of personality characteristics that differentiates us from others, those who achieve success do share certain commonalities. Those people who are living their purpose aren't all that different from those who are living humdrum lives, except in one crucial way. They have a drive in their belly that keeps them going in the face of any difficulties – they make no excuses. They are possibility people. They think "what if?" and "why not?" and then they go out into the world and make it happen.

These former Miss Americas are realists as well as dreamers. They research the steps they must take, find the resources they need, develop contingency plans to handle the unexpected and set timelines. They envision their future and then they do what they must to make it happen. You can too.

What sets successful people apart?

Some successful people might be really smart, or socially well connected, or have family money to help them along. But sometimes those with the appearance of success are often bereft and impoverished internally.

"Everybody is an ordinary person. Everybody! That's what people forget," commented Tara Holland (1997). "I've met a lot of famous people and they're not all great. Some are sad, or alcoholic. Their family life is in shambles. They may be thin, but their body is a mess. You may have a lot of zeros in your checking account, but that doesn't make you extraordinary. That just means you have a lot of money."

Successful people are just ordinary people doing extraordinary things that matter to them. They are intrepid explorers who travel through a universe of options and alternatives. If success is a choice, then they make great choices. They are "yes" people.

They have a powerful, compelling dream.

Inspiration strikes in many ways – and sometimes it creeps up on you. Successful people focus on the heat that lights their fire, on the outcomes they want to achieve, then they go out and do what others said couldn't be done. Some confluence of factors ignites their passion. At some point that enthusiasm takes on a life of its own that cannot be denied. They don't want to regret never having tried because someone said it wasn't possible. They are compelled to act by the very power of their passion.

After she was injured in a car accident in the ninth grade, Deidre Downs (2005) was intrigued by the possibility of being a physician. As she recuperated from a shattered leg and two surgeries, she was comforted and impressed by her doctor and began to examine what she wanted to do with her life. She was fascinated by what she learned through her recovery and decided she wanted to make a difference in peoples' lives. But her single mom couldn't afford to send her to medical school on a teacher's salary.

"Part of my vision for what I want to do with my career and life work is to be of service and give back. I was always very socially aware as a kid. My mom has always been an inspiration to me," said Deidre. "She told me that whatever I accomplish, I have an obligation to give back and make a difference. It's not only the hands-on aspect of being a physician, but it's the counseling, the educating people about their health, about their child's health. It's a helping profession. Maybe you're not saving the world, but you're making a difference to every single person that comes through that office door."

They recognize and nurture their natural gifts.

People who find their way to their future don't go too far down paths that are not paved with their natural aptitude and abilities. They avoid that frustration by focusing on the talents bred into their cells that give them the most joy. They recognize too, the things they do well, but don't like to do. They nurture and enhance their inborn inclinations through learning and development.

Deidre had an epiphany after her accident. "This doctor helped me. He was kind and compassionate. I recognized those attributes of what it took to be a doctor and to have that career. I felt that my talents were congruent with becoming one. I saw myself doing that. I would be working with people every day."

As a teenager, she spent time following a doctor around to see what he did and volunteered at a camp for kids with cancer. Her work at the camp confirmed her dream for herself. "Those kids are unbelievable. These kids suffer more adversity than most adults ever go through. They just had that spirit and that resilience. I don't think anybody that works with or sees those kids, talks to those kids for five minutes can walk away without being changed. I know I was."

They are committed to achieving that dream.

True success comes from being willing to don work clothes and break a sweat. People who follow their dreams know that they must commit from the deepest part of their souls to make it happen, even on the days when their motivational dial is hovering just above zero. They are willing to pay the price – in learning, in setting priorities, in powering through their own inertia and resistance. They understand it's the everyday choices they make that impel them toward success or failure. They also understand that, though others can help them along the way, no one can walk that road for them.

Determined to find a way to fulfill her aspirations to become a patient-focused physician, Deidre looked for ways to fund her education. When she found out that she could win scholarship money just by participating in the Miss America system, she saw the potential to pay for college and medical school. "You've got to have a real drive internally and a real desire to achieve that goal to make it through the rough times. I competed for five years for Miss Alabama, and initially I did it for the scholarship money, but it also got to a point where I really wanted to be Miss Alabama. It became a challenge. Even though I was disappointed every year, I kept at it. My vision was long term."

She was disciplined and focused in her efforts and moved up in the rankings every year. In spite of the visible failure of losing several competitions, she won every time she competed because she added to the financial resources she needed to pursue her ultimate goal.

They accept that change and flexibility are their partners.

Winners keep an open mind about possibilities and alternative paths to their future. In doing so, they recognize opportunities others miss. They take the time to study and learn. They are open to suggestions, new ideas, information and change, rather than thinking that they know everything or that everything should be as it always has been.

Deidre, a strong athlete growing up, had just made her high school varsity volleyball team when the accident occurred. Now she was on crutches and out for the season. "My goal had been to get a volleyball scholarship to college, which I did. But at the time of the accident they weren't sure if I was going to be able to keep playing. Over the next couple of years I had two surgeries."

Deidre realized during her freshman year at college that she didn't want to commit her life to volleyball for four years. She had already sacrificed a lot in high school in terms of her social life, academics and other activities. "We'd miss a lot of school, traveling all around. It was a very serious commitment. When I got to college, my world expanded. I saw other students involved in sorority and student government. There were just other things out there that I wanted to try. So I resigned from the volleyball team." Once she lost her full tuition volleyball scholarship she had no way to pay for school. That's when she started competing in pageants.

She used that flexible attitude to insure that, either way, she would win when she went off to the Pageant. "I just thought that if I could get enough scholarship money to get a laptop computer before I start medical school, then I'll be happy. I'll just go and do my best. I actually had put a deposit down on an apartment and everything for school. So either way, I was going to be okay. Just having a back-up plan really took a lot of pressure off of me and helped me do what I needed to do – go out there and do my best without worrying about results."

They see themselves as responsible for their destiny.

By accepting that they are responsible for what happens, people who succeed focus their energy and are disciplined in taking the actions necessary to move their goals forward. They don't play the blame game and or dip into the pity pot. Not one of them sees herself as a victim. They don't allow themselves to get sidetracked, at least not for long.

"At first, honestly, I didn't even look at Miss America. Miss Alabama is a big deal here. In my fourth year, I was first runner-up and I was so close. At first I thought I wasn't going to compete again after that year, no matter what. For about a week I was pretty down. Then I looked in the mirror and said, 'You really wanted this for so long and you got so close. You can't give up now. So I did it again."

Deidre knew that she was the one ultimately responsible for her success, so she kicked her preparation into high gear. "I was going to do whatever I could to be the best I could be in every category that I competed in. I promised myself I would give one hundred and ten percent." In her fifth year of competing, Deidre won the Miss Alabama pageant and then went on to become Miss America. She was able to fully fund her medical education.

They make a plan.

Too many people spend more time planning a vacation or their weekends then they do planning the rest of their lives. Rather than be deliberate about constructing their future, they let the winds of chance sweep them toward any point on the compass.

Having a lofty goal is a big undertaking and can feel overwhelming. People who achieve their goals understand that the only way to make the process less daunting is to break it down into steps that they can take that very day. It's the small steps that eventually get us to where we want to go.

Deidre explored the requirements of participation and then committed herself to prepare for the Pageant. "I was always setting these little goals. I would break a goal into achievable steps that would get me to it. I've learned that I have to have a clear plan of action to get there. The third year I came up with the idea for a car tag [to raise money for cancer research] and I did a lot of work on my platform. It was a difficult process, getting the legislature to approve it and all, but they did and eventually I was able to raise a lot of money that way. That gave me more to talk about in my interview. Then in the fourth year when I really wanted to win, I kicked it into high gear. I changed my song and worked with my vocal coach. I practiced interviewing. I made notes. I did a lot more public speaking and performing. It really changed my thinking from 'maybe', to knowing that I could be Miss Alabama."

They walk through their fear.

Those who continue down unknown paths toward their hopes understand that, regardless of the white knuckle terror they may sometimes feel about what is around the next bend, such fear is a prelude to growth. They discover strengths they didn't know they had and that it was a rare instance when their worst fears were realized.

By working to overcome the fears that hold many people back, they risk failure, rejection, and appearing foolish. They accept that such possibilities are part of the process. It doesn't mean that they aren't afraid. They just do that fearsome thing anyway. When they keep walking through their fear, they find it becomes easier over time. They develop courage.

Letting go wasn't always easy for Deidre. "I wouldn't say that I'm risk tolerant although when I think about what I've done, it does seem that way. I'm actually pretty conservative about the risks I take. I don't know if that's necessarily always a good thing. It's just something that I keep working through. Every time you do something and you don't fail, or you accomplish something you didn't think you could, adds to your bucket, and then you feel like maybe you really can."

She tells a story about the first time she competed in the Miss Alabama competition after winning Miss Shelby County. "I did not make top ten that first year and I did not do well in my talent because I wear hearing aids. At the morning rehearsal we set sound levels. I wasn't real experienced at that time. I'd sung my whole life, but never in front of 4,000 people. So I moved away from the monitors when I was performing and I couldn't hear. The key change happened. It was a disaster, the worst two minutes of my life. I cried backstage. I was so humiliated. Then I wanted to prove that I could achieve something like that to myself. It pushed me. I learned after that how to control my nerves and emotions."

They deal with their desire to procrastinate.

Sometimes everything seems too hard. When the urge to do something strikes, many people just lie down until it goes away. Procrastination often stems from feeling overwhelmed – too many things demand our attention and so nothing gets paid attention to. Over time we can be paralyzed by our own inaction, then we get angry with ourselves and are frustrated at our inability to get things done. Procrastination isn't a mental act; it is fueled by our emotions – fear, perfectionism, disorganization, anxiety. It can be difficult to pinpoint the reasons we procrastinate.

Successful folks deal with their procrastination. They take the time to analyze it. They marshal their resources to fight through those moments when inertia threatens to overtake them and occasionally give in without guilt. If they do procrastinate, they don't do it for long. They find techniques to spur them to climb out of that trough of inaction onto the playing field. Then they do what they must even when they don't feel like it. In the long run, that makes all the difference.

Deidre's desire to become a doctor was so strong, it kept her moving forward in spite of setbacks. "I saw myself as a physician. And when I was competing, I didn't win until I saw myself as Miss America. You have to see it and visualize it and be able to imagine yourself doing whatever it is you want to do and it just becomes a part of you. It fuels your drive and your motivation to do it. It kept me going when I was so tired and discouraged."

Then they do it.

Although there is a cost to driving toward a dream, the status quo is even more expensive. Staying put will kill your spirit and deaden your soul over time. Those who understand this take the actions necessary to bring their plan to fruition. Committed to the steps that they need to take, they find the people, resources and money to accomplish their goals. No sitting around waiting for the world to come to them. They don't just talk about what they want to achieve. They don't procrastinate. They act.

"You've got to have a real drive internally and a real desire to achieve that goal to make it through the times when it's really tough," said Deidre. "I've sacrificed a lot over the years. In college, I'd watch my friends playing while I was working. I worked two jobs to help pay my expenses. It wasn't always fun, but it was moving me toward that goal. I had that big picture, that end, in sight."

Deidre worked while others played so that she could have what she wanted. By the time she won the Miss America crown, she had funded $100,000 of her college and medical school education. In the fall of 2008, she entered her third year of medical school. That's one pretty smart woman.

They challenge the status quo.

Winners are willing to risk letting go of the known, daring to change their behavior and environment and bet on themselves. They question existing paradigms and ignore current conventions. Then they make the changes that others are reluctant to do.

Deidre believed in pursuing what was important to her and challenging stereotypes. "I grew up in a small town in Georgia. It didn't have a girls' softball team. So until I was eight I played baseball with the boys. Then we moved to Birmingham where they had girls' softball." But Deidre wanted to play baseball. "They wouldn't let me sign up at first. I said, 'I don't care if I'm a girl or a boy. I play baseball.

"I went out for tryouts and every little boy in the dugout stuck out his leg to trip me. I got out on the field and did my thing. The commissioner actually called my mom and me the next day and apologized for how I had been treated, that they had not let me sign up at first. I was a good pitcher. I struck out this one little boy and he started crying – struck out by a girl. Before that his whole team had been making fun of my team because we were sissies. We had a girl on our team." Deidre said to herself, "I'll show them." And she did.

They recognize the need for patience.

So many people appear to achieve success instantly and effortlessly. The truth is, they didn't. A famous old-time comedian, Eddie Cantor said that it took him twenty years to become an overnight success. Some make it sooner. Others take longer.

It takes time to sow the seeds of greatness. It takes time to gain the knowledge for achievement. It takes time to build the relationships that support you on your way. It takes time to have enough opportunities come your way that you can leverage into the results you desire. Greed kills patience. Don't fall prey to it. Don't settle for less than you can achieve, but at the same time have the patience to continually learn and expand your tool kit. In the long run you will achieve your vision and more.

The very act of preparing and applying to medical school tested Deidre's patience. As a can-do young woman, she was used to making things happen. She will tell you that she is impatient with waiting. "Getting through the pre-med curriculum was tough – that's designed to weed people out. Then there is the application for medical school. It's a lot of hoops to jump through. It actually helped a lot having gone through all the pageants I did. People are shocked when I tell them that my pageant interviews were much more difficult than any medical school I ever interviewed at. And I interviewed at Duke and Dartmouth and Georgetown."

Successful people accept that there is no easy way to get to their dream. Being a couch potato isn't an option. Each of us has these success-oriented traits to some degree or another. Pick those that you struggle with the most. Work on strengthening them by paying attention. Focus on what you want to accomplish and power through. You've got what it takes.

Nicole Johnson (1999) summed it up when she said that the qualities of "fierce determination and incredible discipline" are shared by all her Miss America sisters.

Harness these powerhouse traits, don the cloak of a winner and be the best you can be. One of these days, you'll be an overnight success too.

LESSON 4:
The Power Of Vision

"Once you give yourself permission to think about things which are obviously impossible, you are on your way to shaping your future." Joel Barker, futurist and author

You can write your life story, be the star, heroine and the producer of your own blockbuster epic. Or you can be a sidebar in a tabloid magazine that someone else writes. Which is it to be?

The women who became Miss America figured out how to mobilize the most awesome power to pull them toward their future. It's free and available to everyone. When you craft your hopes into a concrete vision and imprint that mental picture on the back of your eyelids so that you see it every time you blink, sooner or later when you open your eyes, you find your aspirations have become reality.

A vision is that compelling, irresistible and inspiring picture of a desired future that all high achievers create for themselves. Rather than let the winds of the world dictate where they end up, they choose their destination and design their tomorrows.

In high school, Jean Bartel (1943) wrote an essay about what she wanted to be when she grew up. Even though she spent her entire childhood in California, she envisioned her career 3,000 miles away on the Great White Way in New York. "I always dreamed about singing on Broadway and starring in a Broadway show. When I was asked to enter the Miss San Francisco pageant, I realized that it could be my path to New York. I thought that by participating I would be exposed to directors and agents I might not otherwise meet. One of the judges at that first pageant was a Broadway producer. Even if I didn't win, at least I would get to audition for him."

But win she did and spent the next several decades traveling and performing around the world, satisfying both her wanderlust and her desire to be on the stage. Ten years after becoming Miss America, Jean became the first of her Miss America sisters to appear in a production on the Great White Way. It was an unusual life for a single woman in the 1940s and 50s. Her title took her places she could only imagine as a starry-eyed girl, appearing before crown princes and heads of state, invited into their tents and great halls. She loved traveling so much that she started a travel agency, which she ran until she was in her 70s.

Having a dream, by its very nature, means a belief in the future. To make tomorrow today, you have to bring your aspirations into the present. You do that by giving it substance every day.

As a college student, Donna Axum (1964) taped her own inspiring words on her mirror. "Allow nothing to discourage or deter you. Define your goal then live it, sleep it, dream it – keep on and on, and it will be yours." Reading it every morning on her way to class gave her the motivation to pursue her hoped-for goals through thickets of uncertainty and the quicksand of doubt.

Many people suffer from a poverty of aspirations. They are spectators to their own life, allowing the world, events and circumstances to determine how they live and what happens to them. They end up resentful and resigned to living vicariously through others, always on the sidelines, waving them along. Though they see others being successful, they can't imagine it for themselves. It's been so long since they designed their own destiny that they don't even know what they want any longer.

What would you do if you knew you could not fail?

We have been conditioned, both positively and negatively, by the culture we grow up in, the media we are bombarded with, the opinions of our family and friends, our faith and society. If you ignored all these constraints and the many limits they impose, what might be possible? If all the obstacles melted away, if every opportunity was available to you, where would your heart take you? Most perceived limitations are self-imposed. If there are no limits to your aspirations, you have no excuses.

Like the women who compete for Miss America, you don't have to take the limits of other people's vision for you as your own. Eleanor Roosevelt said, "No one can make you feel inferior without your consent."

As a teenager Donna felt that she was always different from her friends. "I was never satisfied with the norm or the categories we were supposed to pigeonhole ourselves into. My mother would tell me that when I go to college I would need to study to become either a secretary, a teacher, or maybe a nurse. Those were the roles she was familiar with and that were prominent among women in our society when I graduated from high school in 1959. I told her that I wasn't really interested. That's kind of boring for me. I'm much more artistic and creative."

Donna wanted to explore the then budding industry of television. She studied speech, drama, radio, television and film at the University of Arkansas. Those areas of study were so foreign to her parents and Donna so sure of her vision, that they threw up their hands and ceded her victory. Donna lived out her early ambitions for her future, hosting her own television show for seven years and performing around the country.

Some people are fortunate to have a clear vision of what they want to achieve early in life. Many Miss Americas discovered their passion at a young age.

Even in grade school Lee Meriwether's (1955) delight in acting revealed itself and was the seed of her lifelong focus. She pursued a life in the theater because any other vocation paled in comparison. "I loved acting. I always did. Even as a kid I would make up stories and act them out. I would recreate movies that I saw for my chums at school. I remember drawing a face in the dirt in the school yard – it was very rural, we didn't have concrete – and had a scene with this downed flyer. I was the nurse. I must have been good. The kids applauded." Her talent and the strength of her vision have kept her in the spotlight for decades. In her seventies she is still pursuing her craft.

Jennifer Berry (2006) also started writing her own script when she was barely out of toddlerhood. "When I was little we always watched

Miss America. My older sister and I would climb into bed with my mom to watch. My grandfather got us shirts when we were newborn and he had embroidered on mine 'Miss America 2003' when I would be 20. My sister's read 1999. Miss America was a role model for us. When I was four or five, my sister and I would go into the utility room, next to the washer and dryer, put on my mom's high heels and play Miss America. Somehow I always got to be Miss America. My sister to this day says that when she tried to be Miss America and I was supposed to be the master of ceremonies, I just walked away and said I didn't want to play anymore. So even at that age, it seemed I wanted to be Miss America."

Having a vision for yourself will inspire you at any stage of your life. Sometimes you go down a different path as life events clarify your direction. It's never too early or too late to fulfill a longing or find your purpose. Regardless of your circumstances, you can reach beyond your own real limits to do what seems impossible.

Mary Ann Mobley (1959) credits World Vision, a global relief organization, for igniting her passion to document the plight of women and children in third-world countries and tell the world about the atrocities being committed. She had a vision that she could make a difference by bringing in needed medical supplies and bringing out the stories of the victims' plight.

After she had done a reading for one of World Vision's broadcasts, Mary Ann was intrigued by what she learned about what was happening in other parts of the world. The agency asked her if she would be willing to work with them to film a documentary. "That was a big turning point in my life. My first trip in 1981 was to Cambodia shortly after Pol Pot fled to the north. After a long flight I boarded a small plane with my film crew and flew to the camps. I lived in tents and ate whatever the locals were eating. I ate camel and the local bread that looked like an ace bandage. I was in over-crowded camps with no sanitary facilities. I saw mass graves and prisons where the walls and floors were stained with blood. I had never seen the horrors that man could visit upon man like that. I went back three more times to Cambodia."

Throughout the next decade Mary Ann continued her documentary filmmaking in Somalia, Ethiopia, Kenya, Mozambique and Zimbabwe.

She told me hair-raising stories about the appalling living conditions she had to endure and horrific sights she witnessed, interrogations by hostile military and government officials and attacks by guerillas who were trying to steal the medical supplies she and her crew were bringing in. She was willing to put herself in a position of danger and her life on the line because of her passion for the cause. "You come to a point in your life when you are willing to be inconvenienced greatly to make a difference." That's the power of vision.

Heather Whitestone (1995) became deaf as a toddler from a severe infection. Her parents raised her to believe in the breadth of her own potential. "I used to dream about giving a speech on stage," she said. "I never thought I could do that for a living, being deaf. When I was competing for Miss America, I had my own vision to inspire people to make their dreams come true. I wanted to dance all the time, to be a well-known ballerina. That was my dream."

For many of the other Miss Americas, their vision wasn't so different from the reality. But for her, it was. "I never saw myself as disabled. I thought it was a curse at first. You don't want to be different from other people. But time went on and I changed my perspective.

"When I won, the very next day the world had a different vision for me, just because I was the first Miss America with a disability. Toys "R" Us wanted me to promote their toys for children that have a disability. The President's Committee on Employment of People With Disabilities wanted me to promote their new law, the Americans With Disabilities Act that just passed shortly before I won Miss America. A hearing aid company wanted me to have a campaign with them to promote an awareness program and to encourage people not to be ashamed to wear one. Everybody had their own vision of what I should do as Miss America. That changed me. Somehow, I could not do what I wanted to do. I had to fit into their vision in order to make my dream come true."

Then Heather came to understand that the voice she gained as Miss America meant that she could talk about achieving one's desired destiny in a way no one else could. "I learned later on after I won that I could talk to a particular group of people who have an added burden, to pursue their dreams and say to them – I did this, so you can too. Now

I'm happy to help. I came to understand that I have a powerful voice to make a significant contribution. My life became bigger than ballet."

By putting her vision out into the world, Susan Powell (1981) understood that events would happen that would help her realize it. When she first came to New York from Oklahoma, she was focused on an operatic career. After a few years, realizing that the life of an opera singer was not for her, she started studying acting and doing more theater and musicals. Several years passed and "then I just started talking about television," said Susan. "I wanted to be on television. I knew I had the gift of gab, so I just started sticking it out there, talking about it to anyone who would listen." Six months after she told her agents about her desire, she had her own television show. *Home Matters* ran for sixty-five episodes and four years.

"To this day," continued Susan, "I really do believe in the power of your own vision and the power of keeping that part of you, your talent and belief, intact. Do not let anyone take away that kernel of belief. It is too precious."

Though she had been a motivational speaker since her Miss America days, Marilyn Van Derbur (1958) didn't realize that her calling was to educate society and help other victims of sexual abuse until she was in her early fifties. Up to then, only her husband, who has always been supportive and loving, knew the truth about her emotionally crippling childhood when she was sexually abused by her father. It wasn't until she was healed enough, after years of an agonizing recovery process, that she found the courage to tell her daughter and then others about her experience and to use her knowledge to make a difference.

"I could never have imagined that, by using my story as the scaffolding, it would be my mission to educate judges, doctors, nurses, lawyers, teachers, therapists and especially, parents," Marilyn wrote in her book, *Miss America By Day*. "The titles of 'Miss America' and 'Outstanding Woman Speaker in America' gave me entrée into being the keynote speaker for many diverse audiences. The more I share, the greater the understanding. I now choose to disclose every part of my story, no matter how difficult, because I believe it can help a parent, child-care worker, teacher, physician or adult survivor to better understand the scope of the issues."

It is Marilyn's hope that her work encourages others to think about their lives and empowers survivors to free their voices that "have been muted by shame for decades." If her email and mailbox are any indication, she has made a difference in the lives of tens of thousands of individuals over the years.

The big picture

There are many paths to the future. Young women enter the Pageant for various reasons. For some the glitz and the glamour are enough. What little girl doesn't like to dress up in fancy clothes, put on mother's lipstick and dance in the living room? That is vision enough to feed their determination.

Others, with a larger hunger, see it as a stepping-stone to big league opportunities and are not necessarily focused on winning the crown. They enter because of the scholarship money that they could win. You don't have to win a pageant to win scholarship money. A contestant can also receive funding by excelling in a number of categories such as talent, placing as a runner-up or for community service. Then they can fulfill a larger vision of getting their education and pursuing a career. So they still reach their goal.

Many women who participated at the local and state levels, even though they didn't win, are now debt free. They paid for a significant part of their college education by competing in the Miss America system, some for several years, knowing full well that the likelihood of winning the crown was small. But they were able to start out in life without the burden of student loans and with a set of skills and experiences difficult to duplicate at such a young age.

For those who did win, the crown was the symbol of a platform to a bigger world that was now available to them.

As the second youngest of ten children in her close-knit family, Angie Baraquio (2001) knew that money for college was in limited supply. "In my mind I always wanted to become Miss America and compete in the Miss America system. The scholarship aspect attracted me. I liked that the Pageant placed a lot of emphasis on interview. I always wanted to be a professional speaker. It was obvious to me that

Miss America was the way to go. It was that ticket to a new life for me that my parents couldn't afford to give me."

Angie got her ticket. Not only did she fund her master's degree in education, but she was able to help her parents financially too. Her ticket opened doors to a television show with her sisters and appearances around the country. She was able to start her own charitable foundation supporting character education in the schools and an entertainment business with her husband.

Donna Axum (1964) didn't let the limited perspective of living in a small town hold her back. "I was born and raised in Eldorado, Arkansas, which is a small town of about 25,000. There is a tendency in any small town, particularly in some of the southern states that are considered rural, to psychologically limit the scope of possibility in the minds of children. A lot of people think that they can't accomplish much because they're from a small town in Arkansas. I always had a burning sense of moving toward the utilization of my talents and looking for opportunities to excel, or looking for opportunities that fit my aptitudes.

"To define the word success you have to start with a complete understanding of who you were created to be," Donna continued. "If you don't, you are going to plug into the wrong thing and become frustrated or pigeonholed in life and become dissatisfied with what you are doing. I'm a religious person. I try to stay true to my religious training in everything I do and in my values and judgments that I make in business and life. Then you have to develop the path that utilizes those talents. As you get to the next level or you get to the bigger box, you say – well, that wasn't so difficult. You were able to clear away the mental roadblocks that you create in your mind about not being about to do something. Will I fail?" Donna didn't fail and has gone on to create a life rich with experiences that have utilized her gifts.

When you believe so strongly in a larger vision for yourself, any obstacles or fearsome possibilities melt under the heat of your belief.

A contestant needs to be clear about her mission and passion in order to be in the final group at the Pageant, according to Heather French (2000). "When they get to the Pageant, the first third of the contestants realize that they don't really want the job; they just want to be Miss America. The second third think they want the job, but by the end of two weeks, after meeting Formers and finding out everything that is required, they get overwhelmed by what they see and realize that they would really rather just go home and represent their state. The last third are the ones who see the opportunity to carry their message to a national audience. These are the ones you are competing against."

Diagnosed with diabetes at nineteen, Nicole Johnson (1999) was clear about her motivation for competing. "I did not have a hunger for the title. I had a hunger for the cause. I was all about my cause of diabetes. I had a very sharp, direct, intense focus on that. I didn't spend time at the Miss America competition engaging in relationships and becoming very chummy with other contestants. I was just very, very focused on the fact that I wanted the job to shine a spotlight on the cause."

Her clarity of vision kept her calm and impressed the judges. "I was the last of the top five to be interviewed on stage. I answered my question and I just felt like things were great. I wasn't nervous or worried about anything."

Nicole keeps creating new visions around her passion. "My main interest is to have an impact on the infrastructure of diabetes care and health care. I'm interested in societal change in terms of obesity and educating people about how to raise their families in a healthy way. It may be unrealistic to think that it can be achieved in my lifetime, but I want to be part of that. I'm both inspired and infuriated on a regular basis by misconceptions, stereotyping and discrimination. I've been a victim of all of that." Nicole continues to advocate for diabetes awareness, funding and research through her television show, consulting with pharmaceutical companies, speaking and writing. She has won international awards for her efforts.

Sticky notes and moving pictures

Peak performers in every field use the power of visualization to actualize their vision. They create images in their mind's eye of what they want to achieve and then they go make it happen. Your mind doesn't distinguish between what is taking place in the real world versus what is going on in your head. Our brains are goal-seeking organisms. When you imagine yourself winning a game, creating a business or building a life, knowing where you want to go and creating a compelling image of it is a potent tool to pry open the door to your destiny.

The women who became Miss America used visualization either through movies that they played over and over in their mind, or sticky notes pasted on their mirror to remind themselves of what they wanted to achieve. They will tell you how such prompts kept them motivated and helped them maintain focus.

"I'm a big believer in picturing yourself in a situation, whether it's a job interview or vying for the title of Miss America. Then you feel when it's happening that you've been there before, because you pictured yourself being in that seat," said Kylene Barker (1979). She would picture herself with the crown walking down the runway and carry that image in her head, in her car, driving around Roanoke. "I wouldn't remember how I got from one stop light to the other, because all of a sudden, I would have tears rolling down my face seeing myself walking down the runway to Bert Parks singing, 'There She Is, Miss America.'" Kylene had connected so powerfully to the image of herself winning Miss America that all of her emotions were involved.

"During my interview, one of the judges asked me," continued Kylene, " 'how does being mentally prepared compare with being physically prepared?' " She told him how, wherever she was going – to a fitting or a rehearsal or practicing her gymnastic routine – she would find herself rehearsing situations in her head and visualizing pictures of herself. She remembers lying in bed one night going over and over an aerial cartwheel that she was having trouble with, visualizing doing it perfectly. The next day it seemed so much easier. She used this technique as an award-winning twirler and gymnast long before she became Miss America.

When you create a mental picture of your dream, you activate your creative subconscious. All kinds of ideas about how to make it real come to you and fuel your motivation. That picture in your head and the belief in your heart make you an opportunity magnet that attracts the people and resources and keep you going when the going gets rough. It's your movie. You write the script.

As part of her training to become Miss Oklahoma, Shawntel Smith (1996) took up jogging, which was very hard for her. When she felt exhausted and wanted to stop and drop, she chased her dream "It's a bit silly. I've never shared this with anyone. When I didn't want to go around one more time, I would visualize the crown right in front of me. I was chasing it. It was my symbol of achievement."

Marilyn Van Derbur (1958) uses visualization to conquer her fears. "I never went anywhere as Miss America that I hadn't been to before in my mind. There were no surprises for me. If I walked into a Rotary meeting, I had walked into it a hundred times. There isn't any gathering you could imagine where I had not visualized myself walking up, taking the microphone and making opening remarks. I'm sure my chaperone must have wondered what I was doing on a plane, just sitting there. I was working. I was visualizing."

Jennifer Berry (2006) talks about dreams she had that stayed with her for months and fueled her determination to succeed as she worked toward winning the crown. "You asked me," she said to me, "'When did you decide you wanted to be Miss America?' In July after I won Miss Oklahoma, I remember being in my apartment. I had this dream of walking down the Miss America runway in a white gown with a crown on my head. I woke up the next day and thought, 'Well, that's weird. I never really thought I wanted to be Miss America.' That dream and that vision stuck with me from July until January [when the pageant was held]."

That nighttime dream was a manifestation of what was going on in her unconscious, pulled from her daytime thoughts and efforts. She had been doing the work somewhere in the back of her mind and now finally, it had come into play. Once Jennifer brought her vision into focus and embraced it, she created the foundation for her success. Once she believed, others saw a change in her and believed it as well.

A traveling companion told Jennifer, "The minute you step on that stage, you have to imagine the crown is already on your head." Jennifer had an epiphany. "I finally found out who I wanted to be and with all those years of experience behind me. I was comfortable on the stage for the first time. I wasn't trying as hard as I had before. Every time I would walk out, I'd say, 'I'm already Miss America.' It changed the way that

I presented myself, big time. I wonder if in the years past I was a little scared, a little hesitant to see the vision. I don't think I wanted it yet. That year I envisioned myself being crowned Miss Oklahoma and Miss America and something changed.

"It took me five years but that year I had a whole different sense of peace. I think other people can see it more than you can yourself. My family saw it and my director saw it. People who had seen me on stage in the years past said that there was just something different when I walked on stage, a different confidence."

Having a dream, by its very nature, means a belief in the future. To make tomorrow today, you have to bring it into the present. The more real it is, the faster you will want to take the actions necessary to make it so. Before you know it, the future you imagine will be your now.

It takes just one moment of inspiration and then action, when your passion is ignited to change your life. Don't ignore your inner callings. Be the oracle of your destiny. Your vision for your very own utopia will guide you like an internal compass when the going is blind, the way forward just a hint in the wilderness. Successful people succeed in large part because they think big and see themselves in the spotlight.

LESSON 5:
Einstein's Theory Of Insanity

"To change one's life: Start immediately. Do it flamboyantly. No exceptions." William James, philosopher and physician

You don't have to be an Einstein to recognize that his theory of insanity holds true. He says that you can't keep doing the same things the same way and expect different results. Follow the recipe for a pound cake and you'll always get pound cake. In today's fast paced world, change is inevitable. What was once thought impossible is now a daily occurrence. You can either get run over by events or use them to your advantage.

The secret to personal change is to examine your attitudes and behaviors and determine which ones keep you stuck, then do something about it. So simple, yet so hard. Habits can be tough to break. Significant effort will be required to excise that old fixed way of thinking in order to move in a different direction.

The women who compete in the Miss America pageant system understand that to get beyond being a runner-up, they have to analyze their own performance and the attitudes that hold them back. Then they need to be open to altering how they respond and to make the changes necessary to succeed. They recognize that not accepting the need to change is a risky strategy. Rather than let change be forced on them, they embrace it.

Donna Axum (1964) uses the analogy of the little engine that could. "You have to build up speed and keep going to get over the mountain. Once you've reached the top, the next hurdle doesn't seem nearly as difficult to jump. The ability to break out of the mental prison of one's own making holds so many people back from accomplishing their goals, achieving success, or overcoming illness or adversity. You've got a choice. You either do it or you don't."

You can talk about going back to school, getting a new job or losing weight until you're out of air, but until you walk through that classroom door, or write your resume, or close the refrigerator and your mouth, none of those desired states will happen.

There is no road map to bring about change. You can start any time, any place. It's never too late. When you shake things up, even just a little bit, amazing stuff starts to happen.

The butterfly effect

In 1960, Edward Lorenz, an American mathematician and meteorologist, discovered that microscopic alterations in his calculations of the weather forecast changed the predicted outcome dramatically. He wondered if that meant that a butterfly flapping its wings in Brazil could cause a tornado in Texas. Small changes in one part of the world can have a huge effect elsewhere.

Any action you take or decision you make, no matter how minute, has the potential to alter the course of your life and put you in either a place of joy and accomplishment or depression and defeat. A ship at sea can vary its course by a fraction of a degree and, over time, end up at a destination a thousand miles from where it would have landed if it had stayed its original course. So even if you have been on a downward slope in your life or just stuck in place, making one small positive change can put you in a very different neighborhood a year or two or three from now. Renovating your mind-set to say no to a negative influence or yes to someone offering a hand can make the difference.

Rebecca King (1974), an attorney, understands the butterfly effect. When she talks to young people she tells them that "the choices they make now will impact their future. I go to court with kids who come to me. They may have minor possession or driving issues, or curfew violations. We talk about the decisions they make and the impact those choices may have on the rest of their life. It will be on their record somewhere. I talk to them about My Space and Facebook. I tell them to think twice before they do something that may haunt them later."

When Shawntel Smith (1996) changed her thinking after having competed for several years, she found her ability to achieve her goals was enhanced. "The third year I went to compete, I was comparing myself to others. I played mind games and it hurt me more than helped me. Going into that fourth year, I relaxed."

Shawntel knew that subtle changes in thinking can have profound effects. "I just wanted another year's scholarship so that I could finish my MBA. It was my last year to compete. I thought to myself, I'm going to give it my best shot. That mental shift helped me focus. Part of that was not comparing myself to what was considered the norm about what type of girls won the title. I'm short and a redhead. I wasn't the image of a Miss Oklahoma or a Miss America. I was able to say I have the strengths, skills and talents that make me special and set me apart."

Making change durable

Making a change that sticks confounds all of us at some point. We have all the best intentions to continue to practice a new skill, exercise regularly or be less fearful, but old habits keep pulling us back. Change requires an alteration of the assumptions that underline our lives and drive how we make choices. It doesn't come easily to most people. Resistance to change is a universal malady.

Everyone is different. Each one of us lies somewhere along a spectrum of risk tolerance, adventure seeking and fearlessness. The world needs both ants and eagles.

Some people don't like surprises. They like their lives orderly and stable. They enjoy going back to the same restaurant or vacation spot where they had a good time in the past. That way they are assured of enjoying ourselves again. They stay in the same job, don't seek new opportunities and sometimes complain about the way things are but don't do much about them. They occasionally try new things, but may fail the first or second time out and insist that their failures confirm that new ways don't work. For many the fear of the unknown is enough to hold them back. Stability makes life feel more manageable.

At the other end of the spectrum are those who prefer fresh adventures and new challenges. They get bored when life feels too conventional or humdrum. They are open to trying an unusual dish, going someplace they've never been and pushing themselves to see what else they can achieve. Sometimes their short attention span may make it difficult to stay focused and follow through.

"Change makes us feel wobbly and frightened," says Phyllis George (1971), a woman who knows how to soar. "It's the fear of not knowing. Most people would rather be complacent sitting on their couch and not challenging that part of their life. But I can't live like that. I would go crazy." With an exasperated sigh, she exhorts people to "get out of that Lazy-Boy and do something different."

At every stage of her life, Phyllis has faced a variety of complicated circumstances and met them with a warrior's stance. She believes that any change, whether self or other imposed, offers the opportunity for growth and self-improvement. Her experience as Miss America taught her not to fear change. It brought new beginnings. Her groundbreaking work as the first female national pre-game football sportscaster and co-host on Candid Camera in the 1970s, as First Lady of Kentucky, and as founder of Chicken by George, an innovative food business, proved that Phyllis was up to any challenge thrown at her. She let the world know that she wasn't just another pretty face.

For some people, the mere prospect of change is overwhelming. And so they do nothing. Not our Miss Americas.

Nothing is ever going to stop Rebecca King (1974). She gives everything she approaches her very best shot. "I'm a real problem solver," she says. "There are no excuses. I don't look at barriers. If I want to do something, then I find a way to make it happen."

Change doesn't have to mean a major overhaul. It can be a gradual redesign. To achieve lasting change, you need to make an emotional connection to your new habits and to the benefits you will reap over time. That's when you will have the "aha" moment of satisfaction and joy that is your reward.

Every change effort is accompanied by a period of disorientation as you travel unfamiliar territory. Knowing that the unease and itchiness you feel during this shifting-ground time is to be expected makes it easier to live through. You are letting go before you have a complete picture of what you are grabbing onto.

The managing change cycle

All of us live with a set of rules and paradigms, formulated over the years, which help us interpret the world. We use this framework to make sense of our daily lives and drive our code of conduct and behavior. Within its structure, certain elements may hold us back, especially the mind-traps of restrictive attitudes. We say to ourselves, I can't do that; that way has been tried, it won't work. That habitual way of thinking is the path of least resistance to maintaining the status quo. We've worn ruts in our neural pathways with those thoughts and hardwired them to our knee-jerk responses.

Then something happens. We either become dissatisfied with some aspect of our life or an external event demands a reaction. These two forces – change we choose and generate (career moves, relationship decisions, health management) or change that comes from the outside (snowstorms, pink slips, family crisis) – are handled the same way, by making a choice about how to respond. We can either be defeated by these expectations and events or deal with them in a life-affirming fashion. Regardless of what the motivation is, internally motivated or externally imposed, the one thing we *always* have control over is our response.

Marilyn Van Derbur (1958) focuses on this concept in her motivational speeches. "It isn't what happens to you that determines your life, but how you respond to what happens to you. It wasn't until I was in my forties that I realized that every speech I ever gave, I was giving to myself. We teach what we most need to learn. That was a major theme of mine."

Making the effort to respond in a different way than you typically do will leave you with sore mental muscles. Therefore the efforts have to yield results that either enhance your life, or prevent negative consequences that may limit your opportunities, your self-esteem, your well-being and the well-being of those close to you.

Losing weight is a classic example. If you lose that ten, twenty or thirty pounds, you will look and feel better. That's a great benefit. Or you will lower your cholesterol and reduce your risk for diabetes. Whew! Dodged that bullet.

Donna Axum (1964) is a motivational speaker whose message resonates. "There are two things you should determine in your life – what you want and what you don't want. Both are equally important. If you don't want something in your life, you have to figure out other scenarios of what you do want and then make all your choices based on how to create them."

Going after your dream will, without any doubt, require you to adjust your thinking and modify your behavior. You will have to step beyond your comfort zone. You will have to take some risks and tolerate the ambiguity that transformation creates. Decide whether it's worth it to you. Your vision of possibilities has to be so compelling that you are willing to live with the discomfort you are sure to feel.

Once you decide that your vision is worth the effort, you need to examine the attitudes and beliefs that have held you back. Who said it couldn't be done? Who said *you* couldn't do it? Are the obstacles self-imposed or based in reality? Every time you feel a clutch in your stomach, you have to examine what caused it. Every time you get a sick feeling when you think about moving forward, you have to find an antidote. If your picture of your future has the wings you want, then fill them with winds of action. Take a deep breath and launch yourself.

Rebecca King (1974) expressed frustration with people who are afraid to try something new. "So many times those folks don't have vision. Two of the things that drive me nuts in my business or in any volunteer organization is when people say they've always done it this way or they've never done it that way. If you don't have a vision to keep you going through the tough spots, then you wind up in the same box. Sometimes change is good, sometimes it's not, but you have to at least be able to look at it and analyze it."

That yes-I-can attitude will propel you past barriers. Your first steps may be tentative. As you gain confidence, you will become more daring. Then comes that moment when your efforts seem futile and unproductive. Don't let the self-doubt that is sure to occur force you off your path. Of course you will make mistakes. Of course you will have to make course corrections. At those fretful moments your old no-I-can't mindset will want to take you hostage again. Additional support to stay put may come from unexpected quarters. Some friends and family may hint you should give up even as they seem to encourage you to keep going. It's scary for them to see you change.

"Nobody will do it for you," says Tawny Godin (1976). "Until something inside you changes, it will never happen."

Whenever we try something new, we're bound to have some failures. You are trying a new way of being in the world. Bolder. More proactive. More self-assured. You are saying yes to yourself. As you discover and create a new you, your old identity will struggle to stay alive. Your inner demons will be fighting a battle to the death. When you make it past those moments of self-doubt, with all the forces of your former self trying to pull you back to the sidelines, you will have begun to forge a new identity.

Like a snake that has to shed its skin, we have to discard our old patterns for growth to be achieved. Before it can open its wings to the sun, a butterfly has to gestate in a chrysalis and break through its silken walls to emerge transformed.

When you shift your attitudes into the world of possibilities and start acting in ways that move you toward a better future, your results will put success within reach. You too can be a butterfly. Einstein was right.

A permeable attitude

Our beliefs and attitudes, forged by past experiences and our environment, shape our perceptions of events. But what if those beliefs let us focus on only part of the information we need to make decisions? Or if the attitudes we hold about what is or is not possible limit our vision? Or if the mental models we have about the way things work do not let us consider alternative scenarios? How do we know what we believe is always right?

Many people focus on what they can't do, rather than what they can do. They see the potential for failure rather than the possibility of success. Much of what we perceive and believe about the world was shaped in our childhood. Some of the first lessons we learned sitting on our parents' knees were born out of comments like, "don't touch, don't talk to strangers, don't go there without me, don't try for things you're not capable of or that you can't have." Those little voices still live inside us whether we are six or sixty. Learning to quiet them takes conscious effort and a rewriting of old scripts.

Susan Powell (1981) believes that you may be following scripts that someone else wrote for you and that it is in your power to rewrite the next act. "We don't have to repeat. We are not our families. We are making choices everyday. Our body is just waiting for the signal, just waiting for the cues. You have to realize that you are choosing what you will do with your life."

Research has shown that we can influence what happens to us by our very thoughts and attitudes. Our bodies don't distinguish what's happening in the real world from what's perceived in our minds. If you hear a sound at night and think that it's an intruder, your heart rate goes up, adrenaline pumps into your blood stream and your breath quickens. Then the dog appears at the end of the hall, carrying his chew toy and all systems return to normal. When you believe in yourself, you create a positive energy in your body. Possibilities appear where none seemed to exist before. Be optimistic about your future and you make an optimistic life.

Phyllis George (1971) adheres to the philosophy of her mentor, Dr. Norman Vincent Peale. "Dr. Peale said that you should replace negative thoughts with positive ones. It's simple, but profound – and it works. If you do it often enough, soon the positive thoughts become automatic. It's so much easier to be negative, cynical and jealous. It takes a secure, confident person to be positive. I wrote about that in my book, *Never Say Never*. The fact is it works. I did it through my deepest darkest hours when I was going through my divorce and getting fired from CBS News. And when you work at keeping a positive attitude, you'll be amazed at the outcome. I've learned to do that."

Positive thinking breeds enthusiasm, and enthusiasm can overcome all kinds of barriers. When you shift your thinking, you start a powerful process within yourself.

In order to win Miss Alabama after placing as a runner-up two years in a row, Heather Whitestone (1995) knew she had to change her attitude about her deafness. Because she wanted to feel normal like everyone else, she had avoided talking about her hearing loss as a disability. The third year she took control and made her deafness an asset. Knowing that the judges were reluctant to bring it up, she asked the question herself during her interview. Can a deaf woman handle her job as Miss Alabama and Miss America? When the judges asked her how she coped with her handicap, she told them, "The same way you handle yours. I believe that the worst handicap in the whole world is a negative attitude. Our biggest disability exists between our ears."

Like Heather, Angie Baraquio (2001) also came to realize the importance of how she thought about herself and what was possible. The first time she entered a local pageant at eighteen years old, she won Miss Congeniality and placed in the top ten. The next year she didn't even place. Discouraged, she took a long break, thinking that she wouldn't compete again.

Once she got her master's degree, Angie became a physical education teacher. Her high school students encouraged her to try one last time. Angie, turning twenty-four, knew it was her last chance at the crown. After that she would no longer be eligible. "I lost the first preliminary I competed in that year. I was devastated. You go from that point of success to the downfall. My boyfriend (now her husband) said to me, 'Seven judges are not going to tell you how good you are or what you are worth. You need to know for yourself, win or lose.' That changed my whole thinking. I really had to dig deep. I said that I need to be my best self, better than I've ever been before. I'm only competing against myself. Once I changed my mentality, I was already a winner. Once I was a winner, I exuded confidence. Everybody saw it.

"It's too late when you get to Miss America to decide that you want to win," said Angie. "You need to know, before you go, that you want to win, because once you get there and first realize that you can do this, it's too late. Your mind has already been thinking that you can't. Your mind is so powerful."

A positive can-do attitude doesn't mean you can excel at everything you aspire to. Not all of us are blessed with a soaring voice or a mathematically inclined brain. But with a positive outlook you can use and improve the abilities you do have, whether they are diamonds in the rough or pieces of quartz that can be polished to brilliance.

When your brain is focused on what you want, it starts to look for the opportunities, resources and information that will help you achieve what you want. As Ericka Dunlap (2004) says, "you just have to speak things into existence. When you say positive things, they subconsciously take over."

Change equals choice

Often, people who are intellectually smart can be dumb about taking charge of their own lives. They can be the most resistent to change. Having invested so much energy learning what they know and believing they are right, they resist looking at a different way to achieve their goals. Many people who weren't A students in school achieve success in the real world. They understand that persistence, hard work and thinking outside of the standard-issue expectations of others move them toward a life of satisfaction and success.

Reinvention is like bungee jumping. You can't do it by keeping one foot on the platform. You've got to step out with both feet into thin air. That doesn't mean that you can't ease into change by doing something that is a little hard, somewhat scary. Each success, however small, helps to build a foundation so that you feel comfortable to take bigger steps. But you do have to take that first step into mid-air.

Phyllis George (1971) recognizes change as an old friend. "I know it's not my enemy anymore. I know it will keep coming back to visit again and again to teach me something new."

Many people feel embarrassed about wanting to be more than they are. They think – or others do – that they are reaching beyond themselves. The only one who sets limits on how high and far you can fly is you. Give yourself permission to relinquish your outdated self-image. Shed your shell, break out of your chrysalis, soar like an eagle. The view from up high is breathtaking.

LESSON 6:
Powerhouse Habits

"The dictionary is the only place where success comes before work." Vince Lombardi, football coach

The most successful people aren't necessarily the most brilliant, but they are the most tenacious. Just like everyone else, they have to climb the stairway to the stars one step at a time.

Like them, when you hold your dream close to your heart in the face of obstacles, others' negative opinions and your own self-doubts, you demonstrate commitment. When you try and then try again when one way doesn't work, you exhibit persistence. When you maintain your focus and do over and over that which you must to master a task, you show discipline.

Phyllis George (1971) agrees. "Making a success of something new requires hard work, perseverance, tenacity, enthusiasm, energy and passion – plus an unwavering belief that you have something that is so special that the world can't do without it."

To a woman, our Miss Americas share these common denominators. They believe that you are either committed to accomplishing a goal, or you are not. They take responsibility for their success. Their resolve comes from a deep well of conviction that the result of their efforts is worth an unbroken promise to themselves. They do not depend on others to drive them forward, though they are not immune to encouragement and support. When it all seems too hard, they take a deep breath, then start again.

"Nobody ever sees the behind-the-scenes hard work that it takes," said Shawntel Smith (1996). "They see the dress. They see the hair and make-up. They see the crown. They don't see all the years and discipline it took to become Miss America."

When you read the dossiers of their early accomplishments, you realize that they have achieved more by the time they are twenty-four than many people do in a lifetime – athletic and achievement awards, community service, student government posts, committee appointments and programs initiated. None of these achievements would have happened without their full commitment to doing whatever was necessary to fulfill their goals. These women have made powerhouse habits a lifelong practice.

Be loyal to your dreams

Passion, not logic or reasoning, sparks our greatest desires and fires up commitment. That hunger burning in your heart is the secret ingredient in success. Without it your commitment will be half baked, your persistence will only rise part way and discipline will be forgotten. Your dream must be powerful enough to get you out of bed and rev you up to take on the day's challenges, no matter what.

Deidre Downs (2005) advises people to trust their vision for themselves. "If you believe in yourself and what you want to accomplish, then you've got what it takes to persevere when you hit those obstacles. That held true for me during the five years I competed in Miss Alabama and the four years in high school when my team was vying for the women's state volleyball championship. There have been so many times in my life when it's taken more than one shot to make it happen. If it's worth achieving, it's going to take time and work."

It's dangerous not to do what you love. If you are half-hearted in your desire, then you will be defeated by your own insecurity. When you have a level of passion that captures you, it will drive you to pursue your dream, day in and day out.

When I asked Lee Meriwether (1955) why she wanted to stay in the acting business for as long as she could, she responded, "I love doing theater. I love creating a character. People say it's the applause. Yes, that's part of it. But to work on the show itself – I love the rehearsals.

I love finding out how this character works, what it is about her that is fascinating. That joy keeps me going."

One after another of our Miss Americas told me how their enthusiasm for their vision pushed them through their most discouraging moments and gave them the strength to persevere.

Like Deidre, Jennifer Berry (2006) had tried for several years to win her state crown. What kept Jennifer going was the magic of it. "I was the little girl who sat in front of the TV and watched Miss America walk down the runway. I didn't see any of the hard work, didn't think she was at all tired, never once thought she ever got sick. The magic of the dream never faded for me. When I competed, it may have dimmed during the year, but every time I stood on the stage as a contestant at the Miss Oklahoma pageant and saw a new Miss Oklahoma crowned, that magic was stirred back up and kept me going."

Susan Powell (1981) has used the gift of her voice as the driver of her dreams throughout her life. "I sang at home and in the church choir. I sang in every outlet available to me in a small town. I studied with a local piano teacher who saw something in me. Growing up I did every solo competition you could do. My mother started taking me to Oklahoma City University every week for a voice lesson. It was a two hours from where we lived. There I met my voice teacher, the woman who would be the inspiration for my life. Every April my mother and I would go see the Miss Elk City pageant. I knew that when I was old enough to participate, I was going to."

But she learned that her voice wasn't enough by itself to put her at the top. During her sophomore year at college she entered the Miss Oklahoma City pageant. "I borrowed a dress. I wasn't really prepared. I could not believe I only came in as first runner-up. After that I didn't want to do it again if I was going to lose." In her junior year she turned her energy to singing competitions and won an audition at the Metropolitan Opera in New York. "I was very young and I was winning. I thought I was really on my way."

Her father encouraged her to enter the Pageant just one more time. "If I do it again, I'm not going to do it halfway. I'm going for it," Susan said. "So I went to someone who helped me with my look and a couple of others who helped me put it all together for the first time. The second time I went to Miss Oklahoma City, I went to win." She has held true to her dream and has used her voice as her ticket to success throughout her life, singing on Broadway and around the world. It hasn't always been easy, but the thrill never fades.

Being clear about your motivation will keep you focused and feed your allegiance to your dream. Tara Holland (1997) knew that deep in her heart. "By the time we got to the final night, there were a handful of contestants that could still see it. Others were missing their boyfriends. They were tired of somebody else telling them what their schedule was going to be. They had lost sight of the overall goal and dream. They had been comparing themselves to the others during the previous seventeen days, so their confidence was shot. They hadn't been able to keep focused on what they were there to do. If a pageant girl is in it for the fame, or any other material things, they will be miserable if they win. You have to maintain your focus all year. I loved every moment of it. What kept me going was the greater picture of what being Miss America was all about – having an impact on the lives of others."

Passion is the birthplace of commitment. It is independent of education, socioeconomic background, childhood experiences and difficult circumstances. We have all seen people achieve beyond anyone's wildest expectations even though all the cards seemed stacked against them. Something inside them believed so strongly in their vision for themselves that they were able to go beyond supposed limits.

When you are loyal to your dream you make a promise to yourself. Only you can keep it.

Turn hope into how

A well-thought-out plan and the persistence to see it through are how successful people become winners. Shawntel Smith (1996) viewed her preparations for Miss America as a project. "I had my business plan, my game plan. I did exactly what I needed to do to excel to the best of my ability." She described her specific steps. "The interview was twelve minutes, so I dissected it. I knew what I wanted to have happen. I wanted to make the judges laugh. I wanted them to know who I was, that I was there because of people who loved me and helped me along the way, especially my family. I wanted them to know my passion on the issue of school-to-work. I worked on how I would deliver my answers so that I was efficient and effective. I only had twelve minutes." To help her be her best, she worked with coaches on each section of the competition: interview, swimsuit and talent.

The only true evidence of commitment is taking the steps necessary to implement your plan. You can be a big talker about what you are going to do, but unless your talk is accompanied by action that moves you towards your goal, it's all hot air. The strength of your resolve determines the size of your success.

Ericka Dunlap (2004) will tell you that she had to evolve before she understood the specific steps she would have to take if she ever wanted to stand on the stage in Atlantic City. Having participated in pageants as a child and performed on stage, Ericka admits to having been a little arrogant and over-confident. When she entered and won her local competitions, she thought she would breeze through the state pageants based on her past experience. Twice she made it to the Miss Florida pageant and twice didn't win, placing in the top ten both times. "I was going to conquer the world that first time around and it didn't happen. I had done it before, but I hadn't really dug into it. I wasn't committed. I had to learn that commitment is what gets you to the next place."

Realizing that she needed to be more deliberate in her preparations, she put together a plan and then carried it out. Several years before she became Miss America, she and her mom booked tickets to see the Pageant in Atlantic City. "I was going to learn everything I could. I wrote in a journal every day. I went to rehearsals. I went to all the visitations to support Miss Florida. I talked to people that had shops on the boardwalk. I talked to anybody, just to gain perspective.

"Seeing all of that solidified for me that those are just normal girls that had enough determination. So you get your butt in high gear and read their bios, talk to them during visitation, ask them what it takes, what the experience is like. I wrote in my journal that I will be at Miss America 2005. That was back in 2002. I wanted to give myself enough time to get to know myself and become that role model."

Back home Ericka read the newspapers every day and formulated her opinions. She stopped listening to the music stations and started listening to talk radio. "I wanted to get a grasp on what was going on and understand those hot-headed people who had all these contentious opinions about different issues. I listened to different talk shows so I could become what I felt Miss America was – a young woman who was opinionated but savvy. I also maintained my grades and had a part-time job. I had friendships in my sorority. I had my life but I prioritized things a lot differently.

"When I competed in my first local of the year that I became Miss America, I was a completely different person. It wasn't just my appearance that was different, but me, Ericka. I realized at that moment that I had taken all the lessons I learned from that Miss America visionary experience and applied them to my current life."

Just as many successful people do on the road to their goals, Jennifer Berry (2006) had an epiphany. "I was trying to find the secret to success and it's the same as it was one hundred years ago. It's just like losing weight. You want to lose ten pounds? There's no secret. You get on the treadmill and start eating healthy. But in society we're looking for the fast and easy way out. We're lazy. My great-grandmother who worked every single day of her life looks at the world now and says, 'Today everybody is so lazy and nobody wants to work for anything.' There's no secret to being successful in anything. It's getting up when you don't want to and working the steps you set out for yourself."

Ericka, Shawntel and Jennifer put together their plans and strategies and then worked the plan until the crown was placed on their heads. They use the same tactics today to achieve their goals.

Persistence trumps procrastination

Procrastination is the thief of time. Yesterday is gone. Tomorrow never comes. When it does, it is already today. Time is the only currency that is not renewable. When you make your days well spent and then look back, you have no regrets.

To procrastinate is human nature. We all find ourselves at one time or another not wanting to do the task before us. The desire to do anything else can be overwhelming. At that moment, some mindless chore never looked so appealing.

Resisting inertia and staying motivated are what separate the successful from the all-talk-and-no-action folk. When you find it difficult to stop watering the plants, checking the refrigerator, or rummaging in closets that need reorganizing, ask yourself why you are avoiding the tasks that will move you closer to your goal. Could you be afraid of failing or are you feeling overwhelmed and inadequate?

Sometimes when you are about to tackle a task or do something outside your comfort zone, you may you feel like nothing will do but a nap. That sense of premature exhaustion is the breeding ground for procrastination. It's based not on reality, but more likely on the apprehension or anxiety that is sapping your energy.

Kylene Barker (1979) knows that feeling. "I call it running in mud. I'm not getting anything done." By keeping her goal in front of her, she is able to pull her feet out of that sticky ooze. "I get a charge out of tackling something and accomplishing it. There are days when I feel like I'm running in place. Finally one day, I get answers and it all comes together."

Sometimes people procrastinate because they don't want to close down any options. Decisions always mean tradeoffs. Life is long. There is no reason you can't reinvent yourself at any stage of your life.

Vonda Van Dyke (1965) never had a problem making a decision. "The only way you can accomplish something is to make the decision early. Just sitting around stewing about it won't get you anywhere. Otherwise you've wasted all this time. If you make a wrong one you can always turn around and remake it."

Any decision you make is better than no decision at all because at least it moves you in some direction. If you are heading in the wrong one, you can always make a course correction any time you chose.

Rather than being frozen by your fears, or overwhelmed by the decisions that need to be made, coming up with strategies to deal with them will help you break free. You can call a friend to boost you up, read an inspirational book or make a list. Find a way to break your task down into baby steps and then promise yourself that in five, fifteen or fifty minutes, you will roll up your sleeves and get back to pursuing your goal.

Don't wait for the mood to take action to strike. You can always find reasons to wait. A year from now, you might just look back and wish you had started today.

Discipline means doing

Those in pursuit of a goal make daily choices about how they will spend their time and where they will focus their energies. They too feel the pull of other pursuits, but they understand that these other activities will not move them closer to their long-term desires. Discipline gives them the edge over other talented but less prepared individuals.

As a determined young woman, Deidre Downs (2005) knew that if she wanted to become a physician she would have to make sacrifices. "In college my friends went to the beach. I worked two jobs to help pay my living expenses. I did a lot of tutoring. I worked for the campus recreation office. I was working or I was getting ready for Miss Alabama. So many times when I was doing something related to the Pageant, whether it was voice lessons or an appearance, my friends were doing fun things. All that hard work wasn't always fun at the time but it was moving me toward my goal. I had that big picture, that end in sight."

Jennifer Berry (2006) credits the discipline she learned through ballet as one of the most important factors in her success. "Studying ballet is a constant struggle to improve. It had a positive effect on the rest of my life. I was four years old when I started dancing." Her sister, who was a competitive figure skater, was an important role model for her. "By 4:30 [a.m.] I was at the ice skating rink while my sister trained and then I went to school. I grew up watching a sister who was incredibly disciplined. I learned from her. Once I got to the age where I was competing in pageants, at seventeen, eighteen years old, I already had that discipline so engrained in my soul that it became part of who I was."

By the time she was in college, Jennifer had had knee surgery, so any prospect of a professional ballet career had to be put aside. While at the University of Oklahoma where she was an elementary education major, she was also preparing for the Miss Oklahoma pageant. The university had a renowned school of ballet. Knowing that she needed additional training for her talent, Jennifer asked if she could audition to take a class with the university ballet company.

"They'd never had somebody do that. I auditioned and they let me train with the ballet majors. So I spent every morning at the ballet school from 8:30 to 11:00 five days a week dancing, preparing for Miss Oklahoma. Then I went to class. I always kept in mind that they could kick me out any time. That discipline played a huge factor in not only winning Miss America, but being able to do the job of Miss America. There are no other distractions. You devote your life to that job for a year."

Tara Holland (1997) stayed focused on her goal all the years she competed. "I did seventeen pageants total. Eleven of those were Miss America based. I always felt that I was either going to age out of this program or I was going to win. One of the two, but I was not going to quit. It still drives me nuts when I see girls after the state pageant bawling their eyes out at the reception afterwards, which is understandable. They're disappointed. Then somebody asks them if they're going to do a local this coming year. They say they can't do it again. I guess they didn't have long range goals."

But Tara did and that helped her exercise self-control. When other contestants went out to dinner or shopping in Atlantic City in the days before the Pageant, she would go back to her room and go over her notes, focus her energy and mentally prepare herself. "I know I looked like a complete party pooper. I knew that it wasn't the sociable thing to do, but I had come too far and worked too hard, not to keep that priority a couple of days before the final Pageant. It's really tough to maintain that kind of focus, but that's what's necessary."

Tara credits her participation in pageants with strengthening her willpower. "Pageants develop all that. You have to be disciplined in how you treat your body. You have to be disciplined in working out. You have to be disciplined in keeping up with current events, working on your speaking and your talent. Then you have to be disciplined on the inside, in your mind, on how you perceive yourself. Persistence and perseverance aren't enough. You have to have mental discipline."

Successful people maintain their focus in spite of the siren call of distractions. No Miss America ever shied away from the mental, physical and emotional effort necessary to accomplish her goals. Just look where their willpower got them.

The payoff

Young women compete in pageants for a variety of objectives that nourish their motivation to prepare. Every contestant is rewarded with greater competency in public speaking, better understanding of what it takes to achieve a goal, increased poise and maturity, new friendships and wider exposure to the world. A large number also win scholarship money for college.

Vonda Van Dyke (1965) was first runner-up two years in a row for Miss Phoenix and wasn't sure whether she would try again. Encouraged by the judges to continue to compete, she decided to enter the Miss Tempe pageant. "The judges had told me to find another pageant and try it. The scholarship was my incentive. I went to college in Tempe so I entered the Miss Tempe pageant. I won because I was the only contestant that showed up. With that great burst of victory I went on to the Miss Arizona pageant."

Vonda had plenty of time to prepare for the state pageant and even there her rivals were limited in number. "I competed against only thirteen other girls in the Miss Arizona pageant. So it wasn't like I was a really experienced participant." Vonda knew that she would have to be diligent in her preparations for her to stand any chance at Miss America. "I worked out religiously. I kept putting myself in the mode of answering questions. I loved it when I could get into conversations with strangers and lure them into asking me important questions. That was the one area I wanted to be sure I could handle – being at ease with people no matter what they asked me. That's when I started memorizing quotes from Bartlett's. I memorized more than sixty on thirty different topics. That was a confidence builder for me. If I didn't have the words, somebody else did." Not only did Vonda win scholarship money, but she was able to launch her career and perform all over the country for the next seventeen years.

All of the Formers reap the reward of success through their disciplined approach and steadfast determination. They share similar philosophies.

"Focus is a huge part of preparation," says Donna Axum (1964). "My sorority sisters played bridge. I wasn't going to waste time playing cards. I was always at the rehearsal hall taking voice lessons. The second time I competed for Miss Arkansas there was a tie for first place. My first runner-up and I had the same number of points initially. The auditor broke the tie by choosing the contestant with the most number of points in talent. I had two more points than my first runner-up, because talent was such a heavy percentage. I came that close to never sitting here and talking to you about it." Donna won because her diligence in perfecting her talent gave her the edge.

Rebecca King (1974) takes a deliberate approach to anything she tackles. "Success depends on how much I prepare and know ahead of time. I worked out to make sure that I was in good shape. I read the newspapers every day. I learned about the world. Sometimes in college you become isolated and you're only concerned about classes and where you are going this weekend. I was working in a public relations firm [after graduating from college], balancing a full time job and preparing to be Miss America. It's a springboard to the rest of your life." That springboard has paid major dividends for Rebecca throughout her life. She finished law school and has made the law her lifelong vocation.

There may be days when you feel like you have done nothing. Yet if you practice discipline daily, the cumulative effect of your actions will move you closer to your dream. When you read ten pages of a three-hundred page book every day, by the end of a year you will have read twelve books. When you commit to walking an extra five hundred steps a day, you will have walked eighty more miles that year. When you take a course or two a semester, in a handful of years you will have your master's degree. Small steps can ultimately lead to big results. A new daily discipline will turn into a habit over time and habits are what keep you going. Then you will look back and be amazed at the magnitude of what you have accomplished.

Whether the payoff is the walk down the runway, that graduate degree, a longed-for promotion or an introduction to a Hollywood producer, the way to get there is the same. Work, then work some more, even when your desire is at a low ebb. That's what winners do. The payoff is worth it.

Nurture patience

What if you gave up the day before you reached your goal? Some dreams take years to blossom.

The majority of the women who become Miss America compete for several years, some as many as six, to win their state's competition and reach the national level. In 1997, only eleven contestants won state titles on their first attempt. Without patience and the fortitude it requires, the ones who tried and then tried again would have given up when faced with losses and setbacks. Their patience was rewarded as they learned more about themselves, honed their skills and nurtured their poise.

Tara Holland (1997) first competed when she was seventeen and was surprised when she won her third local competition. She then went on to compete in the Miss Florida pageant where she placed as first runner-up. She told me that afterward she was relieved that she had not won at the state level. It had all happened so fast and she realized that she wasn't ready for the national stage. Tara withdrew from competitions until she was sure she could handle the job of Miss America.

When she was twenty-one she got back into the game. She was fourth runner-up that year and placed first-runner-up the year after. Coming so close to winning kept her going. After that she was in school in Kansas, so she started competing in that state system. It wasn't until she was twenty-three in 1996 that the national crown was placed on her head. "I wouldn't trade one of those years, not one," said Tara. "Those women who won Miss America the first year they competed missed some things. That doesn't mean their characters are not deep. That's wonderful if you can do it that way. But for me it took that experience of losing. Most people lose at some point. It takes so much more character to lose gracefully and keep going. I needed further development. I gained so much. Maybe I appreciated it more because of the persistence that it took."

Gretchen Carlson (1989) took the long view. "Becoming Miss America was a five-year vision. I did it through observation instead of participation. I spent time putting together all the pieces of the puzzle, viewing all the tapes, researching all of people who could help and those who had been there before, the people who knew how best to prepare me for the interview. I exhausted every possible resource and worked as hard as I could to try and get there."

Gretchen and Tara, like the rest, know that patience is an asset when reaching for a lofty goal. They don't accept defeat if they are first or second runner-up. Even if they don't place they will come back the next year and the one after that and do it again. Patience when teamed with powerhouse habits rewards those who stay the course.

That quiet inner drive

The women who become Miss America don't suddenly start nurturing their talent or pursuing activities of interest to them when they start to compete. They exhibit that quiet inner drive from a young age.

Phyllis George (1971) reminds people that "we would all be pursuing our dreams, even if we weren't Miss America. I did it growing up in Denton, Texas. I was a cheerleader at Denton High and president my high school class. I acted in several plays and studied classical piano for fourteen years. I did all of that before I ever dreamed of being Miss America. I didn't know that I was grooming myself for everything that was to come. Perseverance, tenaciousness, not giving up and trying to keep a positive attitude are what all my Miss America sisters share. With all of us, the more you do, the more you get done."

That drive stokes the fire under their fortitude. "You cannot sit around and become a couch potato," continues Phyllis. "At the end of the day, I love feeling like I accomplished something. It can be very little or very big. But if I've helped somebody or done something for my family or a charity that I'm involved with, then it's been a great day."

With all that they do, it turns out that these women are only human, just like the rest of us. They too have times when it all feels like more than they can handle. Phyllis makes space in her life to regroup.

"If I'm feeling overwhelmed, I stop and meditate. I go work out. That helps me get through. Or I go scream somewhere. Then I come back around. So we find ways to survive and ways to get along in our lives. We all have our own little formula."

The formula of winners

Success is something that committed, persistent and disciplined people achieve. Basic intelligence is only one of several variables in the equation.

Jennifer Berry (2006) tells her audiences that achieving a high goal is the hardest thing they will ever do. She stood on the pageant stage four years in a row before she won. "Four years is a long time when you're young. There's going to be a lot of self-doubt, a lot of times when you are criticized by other people. Anything worth achieving is hard work. I always said that I'm living proof that it's possible. It did not happen overnight. You can do it if you really want to."

When a new Miss America goes on tour after she is crowned, people look to her for inspiration. Many of her speaking engagements are in schools and before youth groups. Angie Baraquio (2001) shared her story with students about how she competed three different years before she won. "There is a misconception that I snapped my fingers the first time and I won. Nobody has overnight success. People think that you can get anything you want at the press of a button or the click of a remote. The thinking of the kids today is so skewed. They think that Miss America has all these contacts. But they don't know the hard work that went into it."

Angie explained to them that though she competed at eighteen and nineteen years old, it wasn't until she was just about ready to age out that she won. "When I tell them that I was twenty-four, their eyes get big. It took me six years before I became Miss Hawaii. I competed a total of ten times. I'm an athlete so I compared my record. I had five wins and five losses. Every single time I lost I wanted to quit, but I didn't." Angie knew that winning comes before work only in the dictionary.

Ericka Dunlap (2004), like so many of her Miss America sisters, learned that to succeed at any endeavor your heart, mind and emotions must be fully engaged. "I used to think that what really mattered was the song that I sang or the dress I wore and how expensive it was. Those things don't matter. You can wear stuff from the thrift store and still be successful. I knew that I had to do something that I had never done before and do it consistently. That's a risk worth taking. That's the way you become a winner. I was able to step outside of myself and look at what was there. I was just mediocre in comparison to others who had won. I decided to buckle down and do what I needed to do to be perfect. I learned from all those things that discipline and persistence and consistency is the formula of winners."

People judge you, not by what you start, but what you finish. All the good intentions in the world are worthless if that's what they remain – intentions. You have to turn those intentions into action and action into achievement. It's the people who act today who wake up in the world they want tomorrow. Someone will act today. Let it be you.

Our Miss Americas

Jean Bartel (1943) and Teddy

Lee Meriwether (1955)

Marilyn Van Derbur (1958), husband Larry
Atler, daughter Jennifer

Mary Ann Mobley (1959)

Lynda Meade (1960), husband
John Shea

Donna Axum(1964)

Vonda Van Dyke (1965),
daughter Vandy

Phyllis George (1971)

Rebecca King (1974)

Tawny Godin (1976), husband Rick Welch,
sons Christian Corsini, Cole Welch, JJ Corsini

Kylene Barker (1979), husband
Ian McNeil

Susan Powell (1981), Richard
White

Gretchen Carlson (1989), husband Casey
Close, son Christian, daughter Kaia

Heather Whitestone (1995)

Shawntel Smith (1996), husband
Ryan Wuerch, sons Barrett, Bryson,
Brennan, Braden

Tara Holland (1997), husband John
Christensen, daughter Petra

Nicole Johnson (1999)

Heather French (2000)

Angela Baraquio (2001)

Ericka Dunlap (2004)

Deidre Downs (2005)

Jennifer Berry (2006), husband Nathan
Gooden

Pictures of Deidre Downs, Angela Baraquio, Heather French and Heather
Whitestone courtesy of the Miss America Organization

LESSON 7:
Victory Over Adversity

"Oaks grow strong in contrary winds and diamonds are made under pressure." Peter Marshall, pastor and philosopher

Throughout history, heroines have had to overcome heartbreaking adversity and terrifying ordeals as they traveled on their quest to save the world. Like everyone else who has ever been successful, the women who become Miss America have had to face similar tests of daring and strength before reaching their goals. We too can learn self-assurance, courage and endurance from coping with difficulties.

Nicole Johnson (1999) has had her share of obstacles and adversity but, in spite of it all, faces the world with her head up and her shoulders back. "There is a great quote by Winston Churchill that I use often in my speeches. He says the pessimist sees difficulty in every opportunity and the optimist sees opportunity in every difficulty. So many negative things happen in life. You're going to have naysayers, unfortunate circumstances and failures, no matter who you are. These challenging situations create the whole story of how you can overcome obstacles, see victory and then have beautiful things happen."

On your way to becoming a heroine, be kind to yourself. When you falter, remember that the reward is worth it.

Fifteen minutes to complain

On those days when everything seems too hard and the world seems to be conspiring against you, give yourself fifteen minutes to complain.

Then, if you want the world to look bright again, let go of your negative attitude or do something to change the situation you may be in.

You need to recognize that whatever you complain about is what you are committed to. Otherwise it wouldn't be in your life, certainly not for long. There is no substitute for taking responsibility for the choices you make. When you play the blame game, you are ceding control to forces outside of yourself. Blaming acts of nature, a difficult upbringing, your unresponsive spouse, lack of resources or your own bad hair day appears to absolve you from the need to *do* something. It's a very efficient avoidance technique.

Nicole and other former Miss Americas don't see themselves as victims even when life has dealt them a harsh blow. They don't accept that the circumstances they were born into, the environment that they grew up in or the challenges in their lives limit their vision of what is possible. They are to be admired for the grace they exhibit and the role models that they are.

Marilyn Van Derbur (1958) was scarred by years of childhood sexual abuse by her father. She repressed those memories until she was in her twenties and then was overwhelmed by the horror of what had happened to her. More than two decades passed before she could turn the traumatic experience of her childhood into the positive energy that powers her life today.

Her period of recovery was long and excruciating. In her early forties, the pain of Marilyn's experience caught up with her, its grip a vise. She became incapable of functioning in the outside world and spent months in a psychiatric facility. "I wasn't sure that I wouldn't live the rest of my life in a kind of craziness, a kind of overwhelming anxiety that I couldn't see an end to. That anguish was all consuming," said Marilyn.

She knew she needed to change her thinking in order to heal. "I envisioned myself as empowered, strong, centered and grounded. I began to know that I was going to find a way to come through this and to find peace and joy. I went to every kind of therapy imaginable. I read every book I could find. I did touch therapy. I did healing therapy. I did hypnosis therapy. I got through it." Out of that experience Marilyn discovered her purpose in life, to help other victims of sexual abuse find peace and healing.

Lynda Mead (1960) grew up with an alcoholic mother, and has no patience for people who bemoan their fate. "In those days you hid the fact that you were an alcoholic. My mother was in and out of institutions many times. That was tough for a child. She died shortly after I was chosen to be Miss America.

"When I hear adult children of alcoholics express self-pity and complain about all the problems they deal with as a result of that, I'm not patient with them. I just think that maybe they are making a lot of excuses. Growing up, a lot of unpleasant and embarrassing things happened with my mother. I had to learn so many things on my own, all those little things that mothers teach their daughters. It was tough. I had to become the grown-up really fast. That turned out not to be so bad. It had the effect of maturing me. My husband always says what hurts, instructs."

She never made excuses nor saw herself as a victim because her mother was not there for her growing up. So she didn't stay angry at a mother who, in her own way, did the best she could. She didn't stay angry at a world that would place a young child in such a situation. Lynda took the energy that anger would have sapped and turned it toward creating a fulfilling life, raising her children and building her successful interior design business, which still flourishes after more than twenty years.

During her sophomore year at the University of South Florida, Nicole Johnson's (1999) world was turned upside down. Not feeling well, she went to the college health clinic several times without a definitive diagnosis for her malaise. Her condition worsened, but the doctors were stumped. Not until she was home for the Thanksgiving holiday, when she was rushed to the emergency room, was the real cause of her illness determined. Nicole was admitted to the hospital with Type I diabetes and told that she would never have a career, be a mother or continue with her interest in pageants. Distraught, she had to take a semester off from college to learn how to manage this life-threatening illness. "In those first few months, I felt that everything had been stolen from me," said Nicole.

As a young woman, she was embarrassed to have diabetes and uncomfortable that people should know about it. While at a pageant, Nicole had a severe glucose reaction and fainted. "I'm comatose, lying on the floor in the middle of the hallway of the hotel where all the contestants and pageant people are staying. The hotel staff is setting up breakfast and everybody is starting to gather. My greatest fear was that the fragile aspect of myself would be revealed. I'm no longer seen as a strong woman, but as a vulnerable person.

"I thought having people find out was going to be incredibly negative," Nicole continued. "I had to come to terms with the fact that I do have a chronic disease. That was my 'aha' moment. My diabetes had been my unwelcome companion for four years by then. I could no longer hide it. I discovered that I'm okay."

Because she needs to control her sugar levels, Nicole must be diligent about what she eats. The drugs she takes affect her ability to manage her weight. "I was one of the five heaviest at Miss America. The more insulin you take, the more weight you retain. The more in control you keep your blood sugars, the hungrier you are. You are put in a prison of hunger all the time."

Nicole has had to deal with challenges most people never confront. She could have exploited this intimidating disease that requires daily vigilance to keep under control as an excuse to play it safe. The misinformation and lack of understanding about diabetes that she encountered firmed her resolve to become an advocate for education about the disease. Just as other Miss Americas have done, Nicole took the knowledge gained from her experience and set out to make a difference.

People who slay the dragons that show up in their lives recognize that there is no white knight to rescue them or fairy godmother to go "poof" to their problems. Blaming and complaining tie up your energy. Imagine what you might accomplish if you take that negative energy and redirect it toward building the castle of your dreams.

Rising from the ashes

The phoenix, an ancient mythological bird with glorious red and gold plumage, is known for always rising from the ashes of disaster, more beautiful than ever. It renews itself through fire and is able to regenerate itself when wounded by a foe. Its tears have the power to heal others.

Like the phoenix, winners find a way to rise from misfortunes that befall them and come to the aid of others as well. Where and how they grow up, or limits in their current situation, are not what define them. They don't throw up their hands and surrender to despair. They revamp their strategies and find another way toward victory.

Donna Axum (1964) says that "you have to continuously reinvent yourself based on the adversity that you face. That reinvention process is the key element in moving forward to the next level, accomplishing something, redirecting your life, getting your psyche back on track."

One of the most difficult situations Donna has ever had to deal with happened about a year and a half after she married the Speaker of the Texas House of Representatives. The Nixon administration had initiated a political investigation into the Democratic leadership of the state. As part of a banking scandal, the governor and several aides were being investigated for conspiracy to accept a bribe. Donna and her husband were living in the Speaker's apartment in the State Capitol Building in Austin at the time.

"We lived inside the fishbowl that was Texas politics. I was fairly young [about thirty] to be the wife of the Speaker of the House. In January 1971, the investigation became national news. We were on the six and ten o'clock news every night. The press camped out in the back hall. That went on for more than six months. It was a time of bomb threats and a lot of unrest on the University of Texas campus. It was not uncommon for a bomb threat to be called into the Capitol. We would have to evacuate in the middle of the night with kids in tow."

Donna's husband was convicted of conspiracy, given a five-year probated sentence and resigned as Speaker. "Our lives were in shambles. Because I was Miss America, the picture of us coming out of the courthouse was picked up by Associated Press and was everywhere."

Donna and her husband returned to Burnham, the small Texas town where he grew up. Needing to work to help support the family, she got a job teaching speech at a small junior college. While her husband struggled to get past what had happened, Donna was trying to make a life.

"I was just mired in negativity," Donna continued. "The spark that was in me was becoming a low ember. I knew that I had to make a tough decision about my marriage. I decided to move back to Austin, find a job and move forward."

She still faced much resistance as she attempted to repair her life. "I went back to the town that we had lived in. When I was looking for a job, I called on a lot of people that I knew. They wouldn't return my calls. They didn't want to get involved."

But Donna was persistent and finally landed a job with the dean of communications at the University of Texas. "That was my first step at getting my life back on track and rebuilding it. It was a tough, uphill climb, emotionally, mentally and financially. I had to keep persevering and make the best decisions that I could at any given time in the process." Donna did persist and went on to teach communications, have her own public affairs television show, become a motivational speaker and perform as a guest singer with several symphonies.

Vonda Van Dyke (1965) let nothing stop her as she pursued her long-term goal. Although she had won the pageant as a ventriloquist, Vonda had a fine voice and wanted to become a singer. A year after she was Miss America, she was diagnosed with valley fever, a fungal infection in the lungs. The only cure was to remove three-quarters of one lung. That would have stopped most people, but not Vonda.

"I was diagnosed just about the time I was deciding to be a singer. Ventriloquism doesn't take breath control, but singing does. It was quite a challenge. I think that if I had decided not to go for a singing career, I probably wouldn't be as healthy as I am today, because I had to learn all those breathing exercises. There were certain things I couldn't do on stage. Singing and dancing at the same time was very difficult."

Vonda could have decided that her career was over, but she didn't see it that way. She learned breath control and practiced her craft until she could do it to the best of her ability. Her reduced lung capacity didn't stand in the way of a long career in the entertainment industry. She went on to record several albums and perform around the country.

Each of these women was able to rise above devastating events and find her way back into the light. Like others who succeed, they didn't wallow in self-pity for more than a few moments before they donned their tattered wings, lifted their heads and rose from the ashes.

A bump in the road

It wasn't until her sixth year of competing that Nicole Johnson (1999) won the national title. Jennifer Berry (2006) and Donna Axum (1964) each competed for five years; Shawntel Smith (1996) didn't stop trying for four years and took part in twenty pageants. Angie Baraquio (2001) tried three times at the state level, ten times overall. It took two years for Phyllis George (1971) to become Miss America. After their initial disappointment, not one of them saw any loss as a failure, but as a learning experience to examine how they could improve their chances the following year. They learned that the message in each rejection was 'not now' rather than 'not ever.'

Pageant eligibility rules for Miss America allow women to compete multiple years at the state and local level and in more than one state. The Miss America Organization does not view a history of participation in numerous local and state competitions in a negative light and applauds women who don't give up. Repeated attempts that result in a loss each time by the thinnest of margins can wear at one's confidence. Persistence is seen as a sign of psychological strength by the organization. Those young women who don't abandon their efforts in spite of discouraging defeats are to be admired.

Jennifer Berry (2006) tells audiences, "I stood on that state stage four times and walked away without the crown. People don't see the years of failure that come before you reach your goal. There were a lot of times when I didn't know if I'd go back. But the great thing about the Miss America program was that it was paying my way through college and I had fun with it.

"There are so many times in life when you're trying to reach a goal," Jennifer continued. "There's something you want to do and you're not getting there. You're wondering why not, over and over again." Jennifer feels that, even though she failed so many years in a row as she tried for the state title, in retrospect she was preparing to be Miss America. "Here

I was trying to be Miss Oklahoma not realizing that I was actually at the beginning of something far larger. It took that process of failure and experience to understand the importance of perseverance."

Our Miss Americas understand that though they may have experienced failure, they are not failures. Anyone who has not been disappointed at some time in her life is not really living. Those folks are just taking the safest path to tomorrow. Disappointment is inevitable when you aim for lofty goals. And sometimes, something better comes along.

Gretchen Carlson (1989) found breaking into the television industry as a news reporter was an uphill battle on a bumpy path strewn with very large boulders. "I worked my way up through a lot of obstacles and tears too. I had to make a lot of sacrifices from the very beginning of my career. My first job was in Richmond, Virginia. Then I went to Cincinnati and after that to Cleveland where I was fired right after I got married. I never really knew why. That year was awful. For my analytical brain, television is not the best profession because it's not like school where, if you study really hard, you get an A. Making it in television has to do with timing and who you know. In Cleveland they had two women doing prime time news for the first time in a major market. It didn't work. That was really tough for me. I was replaced with a man.

"I finally ended up getting a job with NBC in Dallas just to get back in the game. My husband was in Cleveland. I was a disaster every single day. Some days I just lay in bed. To manage it I worked out a lot. I started running even though I'm a terrible runner. I pushed myself to learn how to run six miles a day. You put a lot of stuff in perspective when something like that happens to you. It made me realize how much of my identity was tied up in my career.

"I did a lot of serious soul searching that year," Gretchen went on. "It took a tremendous amount of perseverance to continue. It's very hard to get another job in television when you've been fired, even for unjust reasons. I got my feet back on the ground in Dallas and eventually my husband moved there. We were there for eight months. Then CBS called offering me a job and we ended up in New York.

"You learn that a lot of other people have it a lot worse. Now I'm glad I had that bump in my life because those types of experiences strengthen you. Tomorrow it could happen again. That's the volatility of the business." Gretchen didn't let her early failures stop her. She is now a co-host of Fox News Channel's national morning news show, "Fox and Friends."

Successful people don't accept a failure or defeat as the final answer. They see them as setbacks, not a permanent disruption. Sure it's a bump in the road, losing the Pageant, not getting the job or getting fired from one, but it isn't the end of the road.

Being a weed

Did you ever notice how a weed seems to find the sun and grow no matter what the conditions? Weeds grow out of cracks and through concrete. They grow with little nourishment or encouragement. Just because the environment isn't supportive or nurturing, or someone comes along and tries to pull them out, doesn't mean they won't keep growing. They send down strong taproots and rely on their own resources to flourish. They are tenacious about surviving and are hard to knock out.

Nicole Johnson (1999) handles adversity by squaring her shoulders and accepting the challenge. She recognizes the importance of making informed decisions. "I tend to face obstacles directly and head on. I did that with diabetes, personal relationships and professional obstacles that came along. But I'm meticulous in gathering information before facing them, so I don't make any missteps. Then I piece things off and deal with each separately until I get to the whole thing.

People who deal with an ongoing difficulty find that it helps to make bargains with themselves and take each day on its own merits. Nicole says, "When I talk with people about coping with diabetes, my advice centers around what I do every day to manage it. I tell them that when I wake up, the first thing I see is my little black case that's got my blood sugar meter in it. So I make a deal with that black case. I know that sounds ridiculous, but for me to cope, I make an agreement with myself. Today is going to be a good day and today I'm going to succeed. Then I set a goal for myself, whatever it is, like I want four out of eight blood sugars to be in the normal range. Then I celebrate at the end of the day.

"Some people would fault me for this but it's too big for me to stare at the potential for kidney failure or blindness on a daily basis," Nicole went on. "I can't. It overwhelms me and makes me regress into grief. But if I take it one day at a time, I'm okay. That's what helps me get to the point to be able to try new therapies or deal with an obstacle. I joke about my attachment issue with my meter.

"Humor is another way I deal with any kind of obstacle. I have this box that's tethered to me all the time. So I stick it on my leg. I stick it in my bra. I put it on my boot. I joke about it. I'm the bionic woman. I've got somebody making me a rhinestone case for my meter. I'm sick of the black leather one."

Nicole usually wore her insulin pump clipped to the waistband of her skirt or pants, but in a swimsuit or body-clinging evening gown, everything is revealed. "Right after the top five were announced, the show cuts to a commercial. During the commercial, one of the judges, Peekaboo Street [the medal-winning Olympic skier], calls to me. 'Hey, Virginia, are you wearing that pump?' This had become a huge issue – that I wore a pump. I'm wearing this long form-fitting gown. I nod. She goes, 'No way!' She turns to the other judges and whispers, 'She's wearing it.' They all start to buzz, then look back up and ask me where it is.

"My heart and mind are racing. I've been on this device for a year. I am so freaked about wearing it. I'm thinking about all the people telling me I'm not going to get here. The judging is finished and the winner is about to be announced. I whisper, 'it's right here,' and point to my thigh. I had stuck it on the inside of my thigh in my control panty hose.

"When they see where I point, they all yell. Then they get the attention of the judges on the other side and are pointing to my leg. The media is right behind them. Everyone is looking at me now. Up to that point I had been completely calm. I knew my life was going to change regardless of what happened that night. I start to perspire. Then they name the runners-up and every time I don't hear the first syllable of 'Virginia' I move over. But I'm not thinking about anything. It gets to be two of us that are left. When they call Miss North Carolina as the first runner-up, I leap into the air and the pump slips down my leg because I'm perspiring."

Nicole can laugh now, but it was more than a bit disconcerting at the time. As a new Miss America, she made sure that no one saw her sweat.

Optimism, faith in your own capabilities and a sense of humor can help you survive any calamity in your life. You find strength deep down where you didn't think any existed. Many of those who have lost almost everything and are able to rise above their troubles, gain everything back and sometimes more. If you were to ask a weed, it would tell you not to give up, no matter what.

Turning wounds into wisdom

Facing down an ordeal or hardship changes you. If you are Miss America you take your wounds and you turn them into wisdom. The experience focuses your thinking and clarifies who and what are important to you. It powers up your drive to live the rest of your life with no regrets, to avoid toxic people and situations and to believe in yourself and your dreams. Then you find yourself inspiring others with the wisdom forged in that cauldron of chaos.

Deaf since she was a toddler, Heather Whitestone (1995) didn't give much thought to the profound influence her hearing loss had on her until she became Miss America. Up until then, she had never felt disabled. "I grew up in a hearing home with my mom, dad and two sisters. They treated me like everyone else. I had been at a school for the deaf. I could talk and read lips. I did really well in school. Disabled was not in my vocabulary.

"But when I became Miss America, everywhere I went, people said, 'Here she is, the first Miss America with a disability.' Everybody talked about my deafness. At first I didn't like it. I always thought of myself as a person who can hear, who can communicate with the hearing world with the help of a hearing aid. I always felt normal. It took about six months into my year of service, but then I finally accepted that it's okay to be called disabled. I felt honored to be a role model for people with disabilities."

But getting to that point wasn't easy for Heather. For a while she felt that she had only one foot in each world – in the hearing world and the deaf world. She started to compete in pageants in high school, in part for the scholarship money. Her parents had separated and her mother was working several jobs to support Heather and her two sisters and to send Heather to ballet school. Heather entered the Junior Miss Program and impressed the judges, who voted her second runner-up.

Unable to compete again in America Junior Miss because of pageant rules, Heather entered the Miss Deaf Alabama pageant. "I had to use sign language, but I also used my voice. I was the only contestant on the stage using voice and sign language at the same time. All the judges were deaf. I did not win one thing, not even third or fourth place. They told me I was not qualified to be Miss Deaf Alabama because I was not deaf enough, because I used my voice. I felt discriminated against. I couldn't believe it. I didn't feel like I was part of the hearing world and now I knew that I was not part of the deaf world."

It took a lot of strength and courage for Heather to find her place. "I didn't want to live anymore, because I didn't feel like I belonged anywhere. My mom told me to stop feeling sorry for myself. We need to go on with our lives, to keep on striving. That's just what I did."

Up to that point, Heather had chosen not to address the issue of her deafness during competitions. That worked against her because of others' assumption that her being deaf would prevent her from being able to handle the responsibility of serving as Miss Alabama or Miss America. The year she ended up winning the Miss America crown, she decided that it was time to directly address the issue. She told the judges she was deaf and asked them to talk slowly and look at her so that she could read their lips.

Becoming Miss America changed her forever. "Because I faced obstacles and mastered them, I benefited, far more than I thought possible. When you face them head on you find that more doors open to your dreams than you ever imagined. By being honest and telling the judges that I was deaf in my interview, I won the local, then Miss Alabama and went on to win Miss America. Now, at thirty-four and a mom, I still go out and work to inspire others. My message is that no matter what your disability, you can still accomplish great things."

As the only African-American child in her school, Ericka Dunlap (2004) became a young woman who wanted to be a role model for other women of color. "I did everything I could to take competing seriously, to make it a dream come true not just for myself and for my family, but for all of the women before me, beautiful women who didn't have that opportunity. I tried to make my stories as colorful as I could to paint that picture for them. When I would go to an event where there were older black women who wanted to talk about being Miss America, I did my best to describe my experiences in such a way that they felt that they were there with me. I wanted to inspire them and their children to know that things can change."

Marilyn Van Derbur (1958) took her experience as a sexually abused child and her subsequent recovery and used them to help thousands of women and men who had also been abused. For so many she has become that beacon of hope. But coming out in public about her experience wasn't easy.

"After years of therapy I began to feel again, to know peace and laughter, not having that anxiety, not having night terrors. All of the worst was behind me. I knew that I couldn't go back to my old life. The pain had been too bad and the journey too brutal. But I lived with terrible shame. That was the last chunk. I didn't want anyone to know. After all I had been through I knew that now I had to help other people but anonymously.

"That's when I started the Adult Survivor Program. A psychiatrist asked if I would speak in front of fifteen people. That felt risky. Somehow a newspaper reporter found out that I was speaking. The story was on the front page of the Denver newspaper the next day. Then everything changed. People were knocking on my door. Reporters were calling. People were telling me I should hold a press conference. I was still turning away from the cameras until the third day. I couldn't imagine going so public. But I did it. I was dying inside. Later, when I went for a run, a woman stopped me and told me how grateful everyone was for what I was doing. That was life-changing for me. That's when the shame left. Now I've become a healer instead of the one needing to be healed."

Phyllis George (1971) knows that by telling their stories about the tragedies and difficult circumstances in their lives, her Miss America sisters make a difference. "We do what we do because we want to help. It helps us heal, by sharing our stories to help others. At times we get a bad rap. Some people say we set ourselves up on pedestals. We don't. We never have. These wonderful women are real human beings who go through life's crises just like everyone else."

All of the Formers can talk about being role models, about being women who had to overcome so much to achieve their dreams. They will never tell you that it was easy to do, but they will tell you it has been more than worth the effort.

Don't lose the lesson

If you accept that difficulties are a part of the warp and weft of living, you know that there are lessons to be learned from everything that happens to us. When you stare down obstacles, adversity and failures, you expand your arsenal of coping mechanisms and gain strength and emotional flexibility.

Sometimes allowing the cyclical nature of events to play out is the best strategy. You have to trust that built into every problem is a finite end. Even the fiercest hurricane will eventually blow through, bringing limitless skies and bright sun riding its coattails. It may have wreaked havoc on flora, fauna and habitats, but, over time, traces of its destruction disappear under new growth and rebuilding efforts. Fighting against it can be futile.

If you become Zen-like in your response, don't panic or take a scattershot approach to problem solving, you will be surprised how often problems solve themselves. Being still in the midst of chaos allows you to observe and process information as everything swirls madly around you. Your Buddha-like demeanor rather than your flustered reaction is more likely to lead you to a functional solution. You find the lessons become clear.

Phyllis George (1971) speaks about always being a student of whatever happens in life. "We all have a dream. Sometimes there is static in that dream, but you go along and take the job or move or deal with what life throws at you. The difficulties don't stop us. We go on to the next thing. Sometimes we need to take a new direction. Often it's even better. There are lessons in our losses. It didn't work, but if you lose, don't lose the lesson.

"With each lesson we feel more confident to deal with the next thing we face. But at that moment when something happens that is not a positive, we are devastated and wonder how we are going to get through it. Somehow, we always do. I try to stay as positive as I can, even through the bad times. If I had to go through that again, what might I do differently? What did I learn from this?"

You will never feel more alive than when you triumph over the difficulties that bear down on you while you are on your quest. "I don't focus on failure or on obstacles in my path," says Shawntel Smith (1996). "I don't cry over things not attained. I try to learn from those moments. I've always been that way. I may have moments when I'm disappointed or frustrated, but I don't allow that to take over who I am. We talked about pulling yourself up by your bootstraps. I do just that. Every time I do, life rewards me."

As you look back at what you have experienced in your life and anticipate the future, understand that every ordeal can be used as fodder for creating a better you. If you managed when the world blew up once, you can find the strength to do it again.

LESSON 8:
What If Everybody Thinks You're Crazy

"Do what you feel in your heart to be right, for you'll be criticized anyway." Eleanor Roosevelt, First Lady of the United States from 1933–1945

Don't let someone who doesn't share your vision for your future have the final say.

The people who try to blow up your dreams come in all varieties. They may be acquaintances, coaches or co-workers or even people you've never met. They may be your family or friends.

People who disapprove of your goals, underestimate your capabilities or criticize you without knowing who you really are, can change your life, and not for the better. By allowing them credibility and following their advice, you will spend your life wondering 'what if.' What if you had applied for that job, entered that competition, finished your degree or said yes to that opportunity? If you had, you might have ended up wearing the crown instead of sitting in the far reaches of the balcony.

People can be unkind

Some people will put you down without even knowing you. They will criticize your appearance, your actions, your intellect and birth circumstances. They cannot see past the confines of their own world and think you are overreaching when you travel in a different universe of possibilities. The Formers discovered that firsthand.

Heather Whitestone (1995) was bewildered by the volume of negative comments directed at her when she became Miss America.

The deaf community spurned her and criticized her efforts at expanding their world. "In the beginning I was the target of so much criticism from the deaf community because I didn't use sign language. I also use my voice. I didn't understand why they were so hostile to me. I was not attacking deaf people. The media picked it up because it was a good story; it was a conflict. At first I felt like I was not successful. Later on, I realized that I was successful because I was helping people with disabilities. I reminded myself to not let other people's negative comments bother me. I had to be tough."

Deidre Downs (2005) discovered that once you are in the public eye you become a target, especially in today's web-savvy world. "There has always been gossip, but now with message boards and blogs, people can talk about you online. I found out about this message board in my second year of competing in Miss Alabama. I didn't look at it for very long because it was nothing but negative. You don't need people tearing you down like that. It's very hurtful, especially when you are Miss America making sacrifices to do this job and trying to do your very best. I had to learn to put those comments out of my mind."

Our Miss Americas have all experienced the pain of others' nasty comments and misperceptions. And yes, it was hurtful to them. Very. But they learned to develop a thick skin and turn the other cheek. To a woman, they looked inside and reminded themselves of who they really were and what they were attempting to accomplish.

As Miss America 2006, Jennifer Berry is still close to the experience of preparing for and winning the crown. "I got a lot of criticism throughout my five years of competing. No one actually said to my face that I would never win, but I would hear it through the grapevine. I would be lying to say that I didn't listen to it. It hurts when people are negative, when they try to knock your dreams down. I just kept on going and tried to ignore it."

That doesn't mean that Jennifer was able to put aside the hurtful things she heard. "I definitely had ups and downs," she continued. "Many times I cried in private because somebody had made a disparaging remark or said that I would never win. Someone once said, 'She'll never be Miss Oklahoma because she'll never get on the floor with a snotty-nosed kid [when she does a school appearance].' They didn't know I was going to school to be an elementary school teacher. At those moments I had to and ask myself, 'Do I want to keep doing this?' For me the answer was always yes."

Jennifer knew that the key way to combating such negative energy was to surround herself with people who supported her goals and to draw on her inner strength. "I was so glad to have a family who was behind me whether I won or not and believed in me one hundred percent. When you go through years of people telling you who you should be, how you should look and what you should say, it takes a long time not necessarily to get over it, but to not be so affected by it. I kept the magic, the dream in front of me. Sometimes I would watch old Miss America tapes and get excited about it again."

The criticism didn't stop once she won the crown. "Every Miss America has heard other people say she shouldn't have won," said Jennifer. "You have to dig deep inside. I believed that I was in this position for a purpose. Maybe a lot of people didn't think I should be. I had to make a difference no matter what happened that year." Jennifer did make a difference, promoting intolerance for drunk driving. and currently serving as a board member of Mothers Against Drunk Driving.

Like the others, Donna Axum (1964), can tell many stories about having to withstand the scrutiny of strangers. She would overhear people commenting on her appearance when she was signing autographs and doing events. Though she would cringe inwardly, she kept keep on smiling. "It was difficult having people stare at me all the time. My parents taught me that it's rude to stare. People look at you from your feet to your hair and back down again. Once at an automobile show where I was signing autographs, a young man and his date were standing quite close to me. They were giving me the once over. I heard him say, 'My kid sister is better looking than she is.' You have to be able to withstand the scrutiny of people from all walks of life. You may or may not measure up to their expectations, but you have to stay very centered and focused and give it your best shot." It might seem like a small thing, but the cumulative effect of others' disparaging remarks takes its toll.

Because she is so visible as a co-host on "Fox and Friends," Gretchen Carlson (1989) finds she is vulnerable on an ongoing basis. "I'm not going to lie and say I have a completely tough skin, but it's gotten a lot tougher as I get older. If I internalized all of that stuff I would be in some psych ward. For some reason, if you're in the public eye, people feel like they have a right to say anything about you. I understand that. So I try not to focus too much on it because I think it's wasted energy. But deep down, even though some people think I'm tough, I have a big heart and I do get hurt. My father told me in high school, 'Gretchen, you are never going to get everyone to like you no matter what you do.' It's such a simple statement, but I always think about that when I read something negative about me."

Don't let the negative comments of others become your truths. Most likely the people who attempt to shatter the dreams of others don't believe that they can do it for themselves. By bearing up under their pessimism and continuing to move toward your future, you can show them the way.

Watch out for the well-meaning

Sometimes it's those people closest to you who may, even without meaning to, hinder your progress forward. They may think that they are protecting you from harm by lecturing you on the seemingly insurmountable odds standing between you and success or how you should act when you go before the judges. Family approval does matter, no matter how much we may deny it. When the people we love fail to give us the emotional green light, it is all the more painful because their encouragement means so much to us.

Others who counsel and advise you are inclined to be conservative in their recommendations. If you do what they suggest and fail, they may feel that it is a reflection on them. They may not always encourage you to take the big risks, even though those risks may yield the biggest rewards.

Shawntel Smith (1996) has seen this firsthand. "So many people – coaches and trainers – are telling you what they think the judges are looking for. You're trying to weigh what everyone else says is necessary without losing yourself in the whole process. You have to trust what you know to be true in your heart."

Rebecca King (1974) agrees with Shawntel. "I'm concerned that some young women who get involved with pageants find their sense of self gets played with by well-meaning people and their true identity is lost in the process. They think that the winners fit the same mold, that we all match the same criteria, wear a certain kind of gown or act a certain way. We're all so different. I would encourage young women not to be manipulated into conforming to a specific image. You've got to break out of the mold. That's what I did."

Some people thought Ericka Dunlap (2004) was overreaching as she pursued her goal. "Becoming Miss America was something that I always wanted. Along the road to getting there so many people told me that I wasn't cut out for it. Even my mom and I had our differences about certain aspects of my platform and stage performance. My success justified my path in spite of the naysayers."

Even the most respected experts may not understand the stuff you are made of. Nicole Johnson (1999) was advised by both medical professionals and pageant coaches, who in the end turned out to be wrong about her capabilities. If she had listened to all the people who told her that because she had Type I diabetes and wore an insulin pump, she should not even compete – much less expect to win – she would not be the courageous woman who used the Miss America platform to broadcast her message of hope.

"From the time I was diagnosed, I was told by my health care professional that I needed to manage my stress levels. He told me that I should never be in a competition and needed to drop out of college because it was too stressful. He told me that I would never become a journalist, which was my dream then, because journalists don't eat at the same time every day. Those were his exact words. That I would never marry because I was damaged and that I would never have children. He actually had an in-depth conversation with my parents that they needed to reinforce to me over the next several years that adoption was what I should pursue if I wanted to have a child. There is so much misunderstanding and lack of information. People think that it is not possible for people with diabetes to live a normal life.

"After my first try at Miss Virginia in 1997, where I had a severe diabetic episode, I went home and went on the insulin pump which I had been too vain to put on for months," Nicole continued. "I got some feedback from the pageant world that was well-meaning. They told me not to go back, that I would never be chosen. No one ever wearing anything that's attached to them has ever won. I didn't fit the image of the ideal.

"From the first day I was diagnosed until the day after I won the crown, numerous people told me that I couldn't be Miss America, that the disease was going to keep me from the pursuit of my goals and dreams.

"Their advice is what actually spurred me to keep competing and go on to Miss America. I wanted to prove that I could get back up on that stage. I wasn't really proving it to anyone other than myself. I didn't win for a long time. But every time I got back up with knees knocking and voice warbling, I was proving to myself that I could accomplish something even though I have diabetes." Nicole's belief in herself and her ability to manage her disease finally convinced the judges that she fit the ideal of a courageous, intelligent young woman who was equal to the job of Miss America. Then, several years later, her optimistic nature intact, she successfully carried a pregnancy to term.

Your opinion about what is right for you is the only one that really counts. Many people will come into your life with the best intentions to help you. In lots of instances their encouragement and advice will do just that. For others, their comments are a reflection of their limitations – not yours. There is nothing unrealistic about dreams that ignite your passion, align with your purpose and inspire you to persevere until you attain them. Listen to the whisper in your heart. You may find that it is more insistent than the words of the well-meaning. Only you can decide who is right.

Antidotes for toxicity

Negative thoughts and negative people are toxic to your future. The skepticism and gloomy attitude of both your inner and outer critics can be as contagious as the flu and put you flat on your back. But, there are antidotes to faultfinders. You can ignore them. You can remove yourself from their presence. You can develop self-talk that counters their unconstructive influence. Just like many of our Miss Americas, you can develop an "I'll show them!" attitude.

Susan Powell (1981) takes disapproving comments and uses them as material in her musical performances, knowing that a little humor can take some of the sting out of those words. "You overhear people in the autograph session say that they never did think that you were all that special or that you're not all that pretty. Luckily, I had this fabulous traveling companion during my Miss America year who had heard it all. It may have been the first time I heard it, but she helped put it all in perspective and we laughed our heads off. Now I use it for fodder on stage. I compile everything into these fabulous self-deprecating monologues."

The positive experiences she had as Miss America helped Jennifer Berry (2006) deal with the people whose unkind words stung her. "There were times when I would hear negative things like I should never have been Miss America. Then I would walk into a room full of soldiers and they would be excited to see me. I would go into the hospital room of a sick little girl. She wouldn't really know who I was, but her parents did and they were so appreciative that I would visit with her. I met an eight-year-old girl with cancer who took ballet lessons. Her face lit up when she found out that I was a ballerina. I followed her parents' blog about her. When she passed away, I wrote them a note. They told me how they had buried her with her point shoes and how much my visit had meant to them. Those were the days that got me through."

Tara Holland (1997) shares her philosophy about dream-busters and how to deal with them. "I kill them with kindness, or I just ignore them and prove them wrong. I'm not somebody that usually gets in your face. When I talk to students I tell them that if some kids put them down or roll their eyes at what they are trying to do, it's because those kids don't believe that they themselves can do the same thing. Their own insecurities drive them to respond negatively. If they could see themselves in that role, then they would be able to see you in that role too. Hopefully, at some point you can help them understand that. But you can't listen to the put-downs.

"That's when you have to go back to your goal, look at your plan," Tara advises her audience. "I heard a story to illustrate this in chapel one time. It came from Dwight Moody, a preacher from the 1800s. It told how he held up a glass and asked, 'How can I get rid of all the air in this glass?' People thought about putting their hand over it or turning it upside down. But it is impossible to get rid of air in a glass. Then he took a pitcher of water and poured the water in to replace some of the air in part of the glass. That's what we have to do with naysayers. To get rid of the air, the negativity, you have to fill your glass up with something else."

The worst consequences of actually pursuing what you desire, rather than what others suggest, are far less harmful than the benefits of hiding your light. When you accomplish a goal that seems beyond your grasp, something changes in you. Little triumphs feed your self-esteem and, along with the people who encourage you, are the best antidotes to the poison of other's negativity. Then you find you can inspire others to shine their lights too.

Exorcise the inner demons

The worst dream-busters are not the ones we encounter on the streets or who sit across from us at the dining room table but the ones that reside inside our heads. Those constricting old scripts and not-worthy mantras inhibit us from doggedly pursuing our dreams and give power to the voices of others.

When you are attached to obsolete ideas about who you are and how you should live your life, your thoughts can constrict your ambition. That emotional clutter is keeping you from reaching your potential. By eliminating those "I'm not good enough, smart enough, pretty enough" dream stealers that inhabit the recesses of your mind, you create space to store positive thoughts.

Like so many other young women who pursued the crown, Susan Powell (1981) had doubts about her capabilities. "I never really thought I was pretty enough to be Miss America. For me that was really hard, to feel that I was beautiful. I'm short. I just felt that everywhere I went there would be someone who would comment on that. Now, when I look at pictures of me at that time, I realize I was pretty. Why did I think I wasn't? Somewhere in my mind I bought into the idea that I wasn't typical. I viewed Miss America as this gorgeous blond, bubbly and fantastic, but it still didn't keep me from entering. Now it seems ridiculous and, besides, who cares."

Still, Susan admits to being plagued with negative self-talk to this day. "I regularly doubt that I've lived up to my full potential. Those little voices say to me, 'You're too old. You're not right for that. Nobody will take you seriously. There are too many other people who want the same thing.' I wouldn't say that I'm past all that, but I manage it." As a performer, Susan continues to go to auditions and try out for new parts. "I know, from my experience, that's the only way. The more I talk with people, the more I learn that everybody has limiting voices. You just have to keep going."

The year that Deidre Downs (2005) finally won was the year that she shifted her thinking.

"What changed was that I started believing in myself more, especially as I analyzed the tapes of my previous pageant participation. I realized that I was selling myself short. I was my own worst critic. As I watched those tapes and tried to be objective, I realized that I could be Miss America. That made a big difference. My confidence grew."

Your inner critic may be robbing you of the success you deserve. What you believe about what you can achieve may be limiting you more than your situation. So get your pompoms out and turn your inner critic into a high-flying cheerleader.

Be your own cheerleader

When you are clear about where you are going and committed to getting there, others' barbs may sting but leave no lasting marks. Your own cheers will drown them out.

People underestimated Tawny Godin (1976) as a twenty-year old breaking into the television industry. Shortly after her year as Miss America ended she became a news reporter in Los Angeles. "I started on the air on May 16, 1977. I was perceived by a lot of women journalists as a lightweight who hadn't paid her dues. They made my life miserable.

"I worked literally seven days a week for close to a year. I was resentful because I knew that I was capable and would work harder than anyone else. I didn't want anybody to hand me anything on a silver platter. It wasn't worth having that way. It never occurred to me that I could just float along to keep my job. It really bothered me that people ascribed less than honorable intentions to me."

In spite of other people's efforts to undermine her, Tawny recognized that it wasn't really about her. "Some people deliberately torpedoed my work. I didn't catch on to it in the beginning. My boss was getting a lot of grief that he had hired this twenty-year old Miss America who hadn't gone to journalism school or who hadn't worked her way up. It was just the idea of me that was an anathema to them. It took years of proving myself. People can tell you that you are doing the right thing or that you have what it takes to achieve that goal. But if you don't believe it and want it, you're never going to have it. You can't drive yourself crazy when you're not what the other person is looking for."

You will find your most potent cheerleader in the mirror. Vonda Van Dyke (1965) understood that people's negative comments were never really about her. "You have to evaluate the reasons that they say bad things, especially once you become Miss America. A lot of it boils down to jealousy. I understand that so it doesn't bother me if someone says something. They're not really jealous of me; they're jealous of the title or an accomplishment. By putting you down they are trying to build themselves up. I have great empathy for that. I'm Miss Congeniality after all. I was well-liked, so that validated that the criticisms weren't about me."

Don't let fault-finders frighten you out of your dream's path. When you listen to your inner voice, walk through that first scary door and invest in your dreams, incredible things start to happen. Not everyone will applaud your efforts, but the power of positive self-belief trumps any mud that others may throw at you.

When Ericka Dunlap (2004) won Miss Florida, publicity swirled around her as the first African-American woman to win the state title. "A lot of people who were not my supporters created a message board on the web. Through this message board they got out all their frustrations about Ericka Dunlap. Because it was the first time in Florida that a black woman won, a lot of people used it as a talking point, so it wasn't really about me. What I've learned is that you cannot listen to anybody else's banter about what you lack or their dislike for you. That's really their issue. As long as I'm pleased with what I'm producing, that is all that matters at the end of the day."

Rebecca King (1974) confessed to being reduced to tears as a young woman by some of the put-downs she heard. She had to learn take care of herself. "Sometimes I went home and cried. As Miss America you get a tough skin. A lot of people thought Miss Texas should have won instead of me. Johnny Carson had her on his show the next week and asked Miss Texas why she didn't win. Miss New Jersey was second runner-up and her people were not happy she lost. You just have to get that tougher hide. But inside I feel very open and soft."

Her advice to those inclined to sling unkind words is to be sympathetic to the other person's situations. "You have to be sensitive and respectful. How would you feel if you were in their shoes?" To those who are the target of criticism, she says, "You have to eventually work through the hurt. It's a part of the learning process but it's not permanent damage. Pretty soon you're able to tell yourself that you're almost impenetrable. You have to use positive self-talk. You compartmentalize. You just put it away and say that's their issue and I can't solve it."

Believing in yourself is one of the most fundamental qualities you need says Deidre Downs (2005). To quell self-doubts you have to put yourself out there, take a risk and cheer for yourself. "I'm a paradox," says Deidre. "Part of me is the critic and that holds me back because I can be so critical of myself. The other part of me believes that I can accomplish what I've set out to do. Deep down, no matter what your self-esteem or your confidence level, there is still a little spark that tells you that you can be something great. Unfortunately, so many times we let other people tear us down. Then that spark shrinks and becomes smaller. So it's important to find ways to keep that spark alive."

As the first female sportscaster on national television, Phyllis George (1971) stopped reading fan mail when half of it was negative. She was a woman in a man's world. Many a coach, player and fan scoffed at her in the locker room. "Even my friends were skeptical about whether I could pull it off. A male friend said to me that sportscasting is a man's job and that I would never work. Thanks for the encouragement, I thought." But Phyllis hitched up her silk skirt, determined to prove them wrong. More times than she cares to count, she had to be her own cheerleader. Then others started cheering along with her. Phyllis spent the next decade doing ground-breaking interviews in the locker room and on the field.

Phyllis found that the negative press didn't stop once she left the football field. She, like Tara, believes that being nice is the most powerful weapon you can employ against the naysayers. "Today it seems that almost everywhere you look, it's considered entertaining to discover people's flaws and make fun of their weaknesses. In such an atmosphere, some people have come to think 'nice' is a bad word. They define nice as the opposite of powerful, strong and important. To them being nice is a sign of weakness. I'm here to tell you that way of thinking is a big mistake!" Phyllis counsels us to always take the high road. "If you feel you could kill them, kill them with kindness."

What makes you think that you can be Miss America? A 5'3" redhead with a face full of freckles from a one-stoplight town of 2,800 people in America's heartland, Shawntel Smith (1996) heard that question too many times to count, just like many of her Miss America sisters.

"I competed in Miss Oklahoma for four years before I finally won. Many people wondered why, after competing for three years and not winning, I would put myself through that again. But when you have a desire deep down in your soul and you give everything you've got toward this goal, then you know you can never give up. Determination and perseverance still ring true. You just stick to it. Stick-to-it-iveness is what my mom used to say. Then you might just come out on top."

If you are ever to achieve what you dream about, you must believe deep in the recesses of your heart that you can. You need to cheer yourself toward the life you want to create. If you don't, why should anyone else?

Prove them wrong

Many of the Formers responded to people who said they couldn't do something, not with a sense of defeat, but with an 'I'll-show-them' attitude. "How do I deal with naysayers?" said Ericka Dunlap (2004). "By proving them wrong. After a while, you can only get so excited and have your blood boil because someone said that you couldn't be or do something. It just gets old. So you figure out the next thing and stop being a victim."

We internalize what we are told as children. Admonitions and negative views can be hard to shake as we get older. It takes a lot of grit to stand up to people who don't "get" you. Even as a little girl Gretchen Carlson (1989) had a streak of determination that has sustained her throughout her life. "There is this little gene in my body that when people say I can't do something, it makes me work harder. In kindergarten, the teacher put me in this group of 'can't reads.' The kids who couldn't read were supposed to stand on one side of the room and the ones who could read on the other. I went up to her desk that first day and told her I could read. She told me I couldn't. I ran home and slammed the back door. I yelled to my mother that the teacher said I couldn't read. If I had gone and sat in that group, I don't know what would have happened to me. There I was at an early age pushing the envelope when I was told that something wasn't the right thing for me." Gretchen turned out to be pretty smart, graduating with honors from Stanford University.

As a child violin prodigy, Gretchen proved the naysayers wrong once again. "I heard that maybe I couldn't make a career with my violin. I heard that a lot, that Swedish girls never grow up to be concert artists. That negative opinion was inside me for a long time. I had a very small hand and you're supposed to have big hands to play well." But that small hand didn't stop her from playing for several summers at the Aspen Music Festival and winning awards. Gretchen carried that intrepid spirit into her adulthood. When she interviewed for her first job in television, the station director said that there was no point in going further. He assumed that because she had been Miss America, she didn't have the qualifications. Gretchen sent him a demo tape. He hired her the next day.

Angie Baraquio (2001) was spurred to try harder by the negative comments of others and her own feelings of insecurity, especially about her body. In previous pageants she had never won the swimsuit competition. That all changed in September 2000. She worked out diligently for several months and, to her own surprise, won that competition. "Everyone told me that I was good in everything else but that swimsuit was my weakest point. The naysayers also told me that I couldn't win the talent competition with the hula, that I should sing instead. They told me I was too fat and too short. No Filipino has ever won, no Asian either. It was one thing after another. In my mind I told them all to be quiet. I needed to stay focused on my goal. Even more, I wanted to show them. So what if it's never been done. Big deal. It was fun to prove them wrong."

Heather French (2000) had a similar response. "Not everybody that you meet believes that you can be Miss America. My response is 'Oh really....' It just made my fire burn hotter. When someone tells me that I can't do something, I get mad."

Early in her acting career, Lee Meriwether (1955) was told she didn't have what it takes. But she knew something they didn't. She was passionate about her desire to be an actor and determined to let nothing stop her. Still, she had an internal struggle. "At Theater West in Los Angeles, David White, who was the boss in *Bewitched* and a wonderful actor, said to me, 'Lee, if you don't make it, if you haven't really hit it good in the next two years, then you better get out of the business.' It upset me when he said that. Then I thought, I'm not going to let that hurt me. I'm going to stay in this business as long as I can. Within two months I had a job and that propelled me into another job, then a soap opera and then everything started to happen. I have a deep-seated, I'll-show-you attitude. It's not conscious. But that attitude doesn't always sit easy with me. I feel like it's a bit belligerent and not nice. But I guess it works. I've been able to make a living as an actor. I no longer feel that I have to prove to anyone that I can act."

Tara Holland (1997) tells the story of a bike trip she took with her church group between her sophomore and junior year in college. The Challenge riders covered two hundred and eighty miles in four days, from Jackson, Mississippi to Nashville along the Natchez Trace. The challenge was that if you ever got off your bike while the ride was in progress, you could not get back on and would have to ride in the truck.

"My parents didn't think I would make it. The first day I did struggle a bit. One day we even rode one hundred miles. Some people would push someone else along to help them. A guy pushed me some, especially up the hills. On the morning of the second day we got to a rest area in Mississippi where you could go an extra mile straight uphill and be at the top of Mississippi. I decided to go. The guy who had pushed me the day before told me that he didn't think I could make it. He wouldn't push me anymore if I tired and failed. I took off like lightning for that hill and made it with flying speed all the way to the top. I was so mad that this guy had that kind of attitude. I finished the Challenge, even pushing others for the remainder of the trip. Don't tell me what I can't do. That just makes me more determined than ever."

Nicole Johnson (1999) gets piqued when someone tells her that she can't do something. "That's a sure fire way to get me to try something. As a diabetic, I was told I couldn't get a scuba diving certification. I went scuba diving. You can't fly a plane. I flew a plane. I take 'can't' as a challenge."

Phyllis George (1971) takes her 'I'll-show-them' attitude and coaches others to say yes to themselves. "The counterpart of learning to listen to the right people is learning to not listen to the wrong people. Use other's doubts to motivate yourself. When others question your ability to accomplish something, prove them wrong."

The Formers' intrepid spirits were evident through all that it took to become and be Miss America. Not only did they do what was necessary to place first out of fifty other beautiful, accomplished young women, but had to beat out the competition of all the local and state pageants as well. Ultimately each of them triumphed over more than ten thousand other young women who had aspirations for the crown. That's no small feat. They did it in spite of the crowd's discouraging words and put-downs, despite their own self-doubts and insecurities and regardless of any real limitations in their lives. Having achieved that pinnacle of female accomplishment, their self-confidence ratcheted up and firmed their resolve as they followed other pursuits throughout their lives. Their belief in their own capabilities was strengthened to the point where they could shush their own inner demons. The crowd became a whisper that, more often than not, they were able to ignore – though not without flinching every now and then. After all, they are only human.

They came to realize that when you believe in yourself, your craziness is the most real kind of sanity. If everybody thinks you're crazy, prove them wrong.

LESSON 9:
The "Boing" Factor

"Success is how high you bounce when you hit bottom."
George S. Patton, U.S. Army General, World War II

Resilience is the inner fortitude that successful people employ to bounce back from setbacks and challenges. That's the "Boing" Factor. It is fueled by optimism, hope and a flexible spirit. If everyone gave in to the despair of catastrophic events, then no one would figure out how to cross the raging river, build the city anew, find another job, or dance when once they could barely walk.

Many of our Miss Americas have faced difficult circumstances in their lives and didn't let those events bury their dreams. They may have struggled, but they picked themselves up, dusted themselves off and ordered dessert.

"Several of my Miss America sisters have gone through so much," explains Phyllis George (1971). "One lost a son in 9/11, another had a stroke in her twenties and had to fight to come back, another was sexually abused for years as a child, and another who was in a terrible car accident as a young girl, wore a full body cast for months and struggled to learn to walk again. These are woman who were truly traumatized and came back. They lived through terrible situations and fought to survive. They've rebounded and become stronger."

The "Boing" Factor

Those people who are most resilient are proactive in finding solutions when life hands them problems. It may take a while for them to find

123

their inner rubber band, but once they do, it is only a matter of time before they are able to snap back faster than they did before. The thing is, they know that you can't spring back just once. They will have to practice their bounce throughout their lives, because life doesn't dish lemons just once.

Deidre Downs (2005) had always been a spunky kid but struggled with certain issues. Like Heather Whitestone, Deidre has suffered from a hearing loss since she was a child, though her condition is more moderate than Heather's. Though she wore hearing aids, she didn't wear them often because the other kids would make fun of her when she did. It affected her in social situations. She will tell you that she was shy when she was little because of her hearing and relied on lip reading. "When you can't communicate, it becomes easier just to sit there and hope you don't look like a dimwit at the lunch table. It was so loud I could only hear bits and pieces. Then I would say something that someone else had already said. I felt like I looked so stupid. I was always easily embarrassed so I just learned to sit there and be quiet."

The first time Deidre competed in a pageant and sang, she couldn't hear the music and was off-key. That taught her a lesson. After that Deidre made it a point to find the sound man during rehearsal and work out a system. If she couldn't hear, she would signal him to turn it up. "Doing what I could to prepare made a big difference in a lot of situations. It seems kind of a minor thing, but turning around a situation that was upsetting and embarrassing to me and figuring out what I could do differently, made it a non-issue from then on. I took control."

Deidre holds herself to high standards and, when she fails at something, she's the first to get down on herself. "I'm the worst when that setback first happens, it's like the end of the world. I wonder how I am going to make it through this. One little mistake and I think I'm not good enough. I'm so hard on myself. But then I taught myself to step back, look at it the way an outsider would and be fairer to myself. I realize that whatever this obstacle represents, it may give me the clues that will allow me to accomplish what I set out to do the next time.

"My philosophy is that you have to rebuild, try to take what has been good and then take the negative things and mistakes and turn them into a positive. Then you have to let the bad stuff go." Toward the end of her time as Miss America, Deidre's fortitude was stretched to its limits. "I had the longest reign – seventeen months because they changed the date of the Pageant from September to January. There are so many personal sacrifices you make as Miss America – no social life, being away from home and under such tremendous scrutiny. I was physically and mentally exhausted from all the travel and constant need to be ready for anything toward the end of my time [as Miss America]. I was susceptible and vulnerable to negative events and comments. Somehow, I had to come back from that. I had to have a recovery period, a transition period to regain my equilibrium." Once again, Deidre dug deep into her well of resilience, bounced back and entered medical school the following fall.

Jennifer Berry (2006) believes that if you are going to be a champion then you've got to keep getting up every time you're pushed down. There have been times in her life when she wanted to sit back and do nothing. She said, "Maybe you take an hour, a day or even a week off and then you get back on that horse. You amaze yourself at how strong you are. If you're going to be a winner you walk through it. Then do it again."

In the school of life emotionally toxic situations and distressing circumstances teach us some harsh lessons. If you throw up your hands and accept defeat, then yes, you are defeated. The resilient let their shoulders slump for only a short while, then square them, stand up straight and tap into their attitude of optimism. They convert misfortune into opportunity and gain strength from adversity. They bounce back.

No sob sisters allowed

People who are resilient recognize that everyone gets the short end of the stick every once in a while. They are able to put a dismaying occurrence or a devastating catastrophe in a broader context. They don't look for pity or feel sorry for themselves. If others have survived a similar tragedy, they say to themselves, so can I. They don't allow themselves to wallow too long in a victim mentality.

To keep things in perspective, many of the Formers remind themselves that, for the most part, whatever has happened to them is not as bad as what has happened to others. Being fired, getting a divorce or losing a pageant isn't life-threatening. When life dishes you lemons, look for inspiration at how others made lemonade.

Phyllis George (1971) counsels those feeling discouraged. "When you get in those moods and you start thinking about all the terrible things that happen to you, you have to immediately do something. Think of the most positive thing in the world you can think of. When those moods strike, which they will, I could spend days moaning and groaning over this and that. Then I look at other people and what they've had to go through. I am never going to complain about anything. No one is going to feel sorry for me. When I start feeling down, I just pick up the newspaper or turn on the television. I feel embarrassed and ashamed of myself. I may have had a bad day, but it's not as bad as what other people have gone through in their lives and triumphed."

In her book *Never Say Never* Phyllis writes about conversations she had with Chris Evert, Larry King, Roger Staubach, Governor Anne Richards and Paula Zahn, all of whom tied resilience to persistence to achieve success. "I talked with them about how they got past the adversity in their life and how they were able to become successful. Michael Bloomberg [mayor of New York City and a multi-billionaire] got fired from Goldman Sachs and started his own firm in an office with one window out the back alley. Now look at him. I think we can use adversity to our advantage to push us further. A friend of mine says that if he doesn't have problems, he's not alive."

Ericka Dunlap (2004) admits to finding excuses not to do something she said she wanted to do. She knew that would have to stop if she were going to accomplish anything. "When you look at people who don't have the abilities that an able-bodied person has, you realize that you're not busting your chops enough. Those folks have real issues that they have to overcome and you're just whining. I think about that because I can whine a lot. I'm inspired by people who have overcome real odds, not people who just whine about them. I see my girlfriends who have gone through things in their childhood that I could not fathom. I see those situations as a setback. My friends use them as a springboard."

Deidre Downs (2005) volunteered at a camp for kids with cancer when she was a teenager. "When you see the adversity these kids had to deal with and their upbeat attitude, you can't help but wonder if what you're complaining about is such a big deal."

Difficulties come with living, that's just a fact of life. When you're singing the blues, try changing the key.

Building mental muscle

Resiliency doesn't just refer to your body's muscles, but to your emotional and psychological muscles as well. The more you exercise those mental muscles in different situations, the more flexible they become. When you keep responding to the happenings in your life with the same set of rules and actions, you wear grooves in your behavioral makeup that become hard to escape. Over time you become more rigid in your ability to cope with unexpected events. Our Miss Americas pride themselves on their flexibility.

The self-knowledge and confidence that Tara Holland (1997) gained during her years of competition have stood her in good stead. She wouldn't trade any of the times when she had to make use of the Boing Factor and the lessons learned.

The third time Tara competed, when she was seventeen, she won her local and placed as first runner-up at the state pageant. She took a few years off before entering the pageant world again at twenty-one. When she finally made first runner-up in the Miss Florida pageant at twenty-three years old, she became eligible for the National Sweetheart Pageant, which is only for state runner-ups. While at National Sweetheart she got sick, so sick that she wasn't able to go to a couple of events, so you can imagine how laid low she was. She ended up in the hospital for three days with a respiratory ailment when she was back in Kansas City. She could barely speak for six weeks. She believes that what happened at National Sweetheart is what strengthened her resolve to continue to compete. She wasn't going to give up for anything.

As the competition progressed towards its conclusion, Tara found herself in the top ten. She was running a 102-degree fever. The talent segment was fast approaching and Tara was a singer. There was no way out, unless she dropped out of the competition in the middle. She said that her voice was as hoarse as a bullfrog at that point. "The operatic aria I was going to sing had a three-octave range with the first fifty-five seconds sung a capella, so it better be good. I was the last of the top ten to perform. I was standing backstage and tried to warm up. I hadn't spoken in a day and a half. I tried to trill, but nothing came out. Then they put a mike on me. It was my moment to go on. I thought, 'Okay, this is it, I have zero voice and I have to go out and sing a three-octave operatic aria.' That was when I really found out what I was made of."

She felt that she had worked so hard and hadn't made it through all those years of competition, discipline and preparation to give up now. "I wondered, only for a moment, if I should pull my name out of the competition. I knew beyond a shadow of a doubt that I was where I was supposed to be. I was there, maybe not to win, but I was surely there not to back out."

So she went out on stage and presented herself as if she could sing her talent. The music started and then stopped so she could do the a capella part of her aria. "I began to sing, but it wasn't the beautiful, angelic voice that I had hoped for. It was this croaky cracky awful voice. As I was singing, the sound system went BOOM! People were literally jumping out of their seats. Nine other contestants who had gone before me hadn't had a problem. I kept singing. The next POW! sounded like a terrible thunderstorm in the middle of the arena." Tara felt like it was divine intervention helping her. To go along with her non-existent voice she had an equally pathetic sound system. Even though she couldn't sing, she danced around the stage, putting her heart out there and very best foot forward.

The judges offered her another chance to perform her talent, but she declined, relieved. Not only did she win the pageant, but she won overall talent. "It was then that I felt like my inner strength, just like a muscle, was really being developed. If I had not had some of the experiences that I had before then, I wouldn't have had the mental muscle to strengthen my resolve. But my muscle was pretty strong by that point.

"When your muscle is really strong, you can pick up light weights without it really bothering you," continued Tara. "I found out what I was made of as I was building those mental muscles of inner strength. Now as I consider other ventures or if something should happen to the people I love, I know that I can look back on what I experienced then and say 'Okay, I did it. I've done it before.' It takes so much more character to lose gracefully than to win gracefully. Can you smile when you're not the one getting the crown?"

Tara's mother said that Tara learned to be adaptable by competing in so many different pageants and by all that she was required to do. "Everything was done quickly and spur of the moment. You had to deal with whatever was in your suitcase or when your suitcase didn't make it to the hotel with you. You had to be prepared to speak before a crowd at a moment's notice. You had to be willing to hold a leopard or get down on the floor with a sick child. Because of what it took for her to become Miss America, she really appreciated the crown and loved every day, grateful for the opportunity."

Jennifer Berry (2006) echoed Tara's her sentiments. "You surprise yourself when you go through a life-changing experience with how strong you actually are."

Resilient people improve with age. They don't let the chaotic events that life is sure to dish up feed a negative attitude. They take the lessons from toxic situations and convert the experiences into something that nurtures them. No one welcomes tragedy and difficulty into their lives, but the folks who are resilient look for ways to turn it around and use the self-knowledge gained to make their lives better. They become wiser and stronger. They spend less time surviving and more time thriving.

Be flexible

Instead of scratching their heads in dismay and resignation, the resilient learn from experience. They ask themselves what the best way is to handle a particular situation and explore a variety of options. They don't think that where they are is the end of the line. They take in available information, filter it through their store of knowledge, ask others when necessary and figure out how to cope so that they don't end up wounded. Sometimes they surprise themselves.

In 1995, Shawntel Smith (1996) was just a college student. "In that world, I woke up and went to class. I came back and I'd lie in bed and watch TV. All of a sudden when I became Miss America I was giving speeches in front of thousands and thousands of people. You're all alone even though you're surrounded by crowds. It's such a year of learning. It was then that I started to realize my ability. I learned that I'm a lot stronger, and a lot more patient and persistent than I thought I was. You have to be selfless and patient and very strong. Those are the three things that I learned about myself that I didn't think I had. I never thought I could be Miss America. It's a life-changing experience."

Without that inner resourcefulness and resilience Jennifer Berry (2006) would have withered under the grueling schedule of being Miss America, flying twenty thousand miles a month and doing up to four different events in a day. She had to mature quickly. When I interviewed her just a few months after the conclusion of her year, she said, "You have to be responsible for being up and ready and prepared for any event whether it's a children's hospital, a corporate event, or a school assembly. You learn flexibility very quickly. The schedule changed minute by minute. You learn to be ready for anything and go with the flow. If you look at me from a year ago to now, I'm a completely different person. I'm happy I grew."

Lynda Mead (1960) sees the value in learning flexibility by facing and overcoming challenges. "I suppose there is a religious concept that says the more we are tested, the more we are loved. I'm not sure about that. But I like the whole idea of being tested. I find that I don't enjoy being with people I know who always seem to sail through life. They tell you that their marriage is happy, their kids are great. That's fine. I'm delighted for them, but they're not all that interesting. You learn something about yourself when you're tested. You may not do very well with the test, but at least you know. It's the tough things that come along in life that are opportunities for you to test your mettle a little bit. Then you feel like you can handle anything."

Phyllis George (1971) was very close to her mother, who died of Alzheimer's disease. "I thought when Mother died a piece of me went with her. My brother and I were sitting in the room in the hospital with her just after she died. We used humor to ease our grief. This was the first time we could say anything without mom correcting us. It really helped me get through the first few days." Phyllis was devastated by the loss of her best friend, who she had cared for over the course of a decade. Humor got her through the first stages of her grief. Then she felt that the best way to manage it for the long term was to make her mother's death count. Phyllis is now an advocate and spokeswoman for the Alzheimer's Association.

Life is full of rough edges and out-of-focus moments. No one, unless you're psychic, knows for sure what the future will bring. As much as we may try to control the outcome of an event or action, the likelihood that something unexpected will occur is high. Being resilient means that we make the best of whatever does occur. Not only do we bounce back, but bend as well. Now that's flexibility.

The role of hope

The hallmarks of a resilient personality are optimism, hope and faith – the belief that whatever happens, things will work out and a better day is ahead. They are the key qualities associated with success and happiness. Resilient people accept that life has its dark moments. They give themselves permission to grieve lost jobs, lost dreams and lost loves then grab onto hope and don't let go until the world turns right side up again.

Susan Powell (1981) credits her natural sense of hope with supporting her through her lowest times. "My divorce was a huge setback for me. I separated in 1998. Thank goodness I had a good job. It kept me sane. I didn't know if I could go on. That went on for three years. Maybe what got me through it were my own sense of grace, two close friends who kept calling me, and running. If I could make myself go running I felt better. Now I say that if that is the worse thing that happens to me, I'll be okay.

"I hear about people who don't want to go on. The first thing they lose is hope. I do have a basic sense of hopefulness that carries me through. Who knows why you have that. Some days it's stronger than others. I know now that life is interesting and it keeps getting more so."

You won't banish all your problems with resilience alone, but with the ability to see past them to a more hopeful future, you will rebound more quickly and at a higher level each time.

A strong inner spirit will carry you a long way. Resilience is part of the mental toughness you've got to develop. You have to be prepared for surprises in your life that will come every day which will run the gamut from a mosquito bite that just makes you itch to an earthquake from which you think you will never recover. Whichever it is, it's up to you to decide whether it is a temporary inconvenience or an avalanche that stops you in your tracks for good. Pull on that mental muscle, remember the lessons learned and make use of the Boing Factor. The higher you bounce the closer your dreams become.

LESSON 10:
Gurus, Guides And Allies

"I not only use all the brains that I have, but all that I can borrow." Woodrow Wilson, 28th President of the United States

No one has ever built a stairway to the stars without help. When you are steadfast on your journey and turn your face to the future, gurus, guides and allies show up at your door with the key. Because you believe, they believe.

On their way to the crown, and in their lives thereafter, our Miss Americas had people who offered guidance and support. Because each of these women was committed to her goals, people were enthusiastic in lending a hand.

"To be successful in anything, you have to be able to say, 'I can't do it all by myself.' Then you have to find the people who are experts in the areas that you are trying to improve and who can inspire you," said Jennifer Berry (2006), who recognized early on that she needed mentors and cheerleaders.

Though your future may be uncharted territory to you, other people have mapped similar terrain. Gurus, guides and allies help you navigate a wilderness of options and offer wisdom and encouragement. When disappointment and frustration sit down at your table, your support team will keep you from crawling under it. They are the ones whose shoulders you stand on when you climb over the wall of your resistance and fear.

Yoda, Dumbledore and fairy godmothers

Many stories and myths from pre-history to Harry Potter are based on the hero's journey. Dorothy in the *Wizard of Oz*, Luke Skywalker and Harry Potter are classic examples. The hero is faced with a momentous, fateful challenge. She confronts obstacles and adversity along the way, often put before her by an arch-villain. At the most critical moments her guardian appears to guide and encourage her, maybe even save her from a horrible fate. Throughout her journey, she discovers certain truths and finds that she is capable of much more than she ever believed possible. Ultimately the outcome is up to the hero and her willingness to face her own fears. In the end she triumphs and becomes a light to others.

Gurus and guides answer questions that seem unanswerable. They light the darkest corners with wisdom and hope. They foster a belief that an exit exists at the other end of that dark and scary cave. Dorothy had the Good Witch of the North; Luke had Yoda; Harry had Dumbledore.

These stories resonate because they reflect what happens in real life and appeal to our higher instincts. They are rooted in the ancient myths of transformation. Each of us can live our own hero's journey.

Gurus and guides

People at the highest levels of achievement have coaches and mentors. Olympic athletes have coaches to inspire and challenge them to run that extra one-tenth of a second faster or jump that inch farther. New doctors intern themselves to those physicians who are doing innovative and superior work. The people who reach the top of their profession almost always have someone who helped open doors and show them the way.

The best gurus are knowledgeable and nonjudgmental. By cultivating your self-awareness, they help you integrate your values, skills and dreams. With them you can share your triumphs and defeats, explore new ideas and find a willing ear. They recognize you for your achievements, cheer you up when you are down and help to keep you motivated. Having someone who guides your choices and provides the insight that only experience can bring is an invaluable asset.

By offering a variety of perspectives about an opportunity or issue, they can help you see alternative solutions that you might not have thought of on your own. In addition, mentors can be role models who show you that your dreams are achievable. Rebecca King (1974) commented, "If you have a mentor to bounce something off of, maybe some of those choices won't be so scary."

During her preparations for the pageant, Angie Baraquio (2001) had a guru and ally in her pageant director. "He was my therapist and my mentor. He heard me cry and vent. I was a little Filipino Catholic girl from Hawaii. I had lived a sheltered life. With seven girls and three boys, my parents kept a tight rein on us. Until Miss America I had never been away from home for more than ten days. Having him show me the bigger picture helped me through a lot of issues."

Over the years you may have more than one guru. They come in all shapes and sizes, some paid, some not, some peers, some higher-ups. By finding and cultivating suitable people as mentors, you tilt the scales in your favor.

Jennifer Berry (2006) credits the comprehensive support she received with helping her achieve her goals. "Before I even won Miss Oklahoma, I had so many people behind me helping me to get there – people who were truly passionate about seeing young women become all that they could be. It wasn't just about the winner. You would see girls who didn't win fund their education and later become doctors and lawyers. They became successful because of what they learned competing in the Miss Oklahoma program."

Also from Oklahoma, Shawntel Smith (1996) echoed Jennifer and explained what made Oklahoma so special. "As with any organization, it's all about the people. The director had a passion in his heart to make sure the Oklahoma pageant was one that could be respected. It wasn't about putting on a sparkly gown and waving in a parade. All of those volunteers were truly passionate about seeing their program succeed and their young women become the best they could be."

Every one of the people whose tutelage Shawntel came under helped her improve her natural gifts and develop what was unique about her. "I never ever questioned whether I had the best advice. My talent coach took my voice to its highest level. My interview coach didn't tell me what I should think or how I should respond. He helped me put my ideas together and clarify what I believed. He never once manipulated my beliefs or philosophy or ideas. It was a family that wrapped its arms around you," Shawntel continued. "You felt accepted for who you were, but you knew they were pushing you to become better."

Many of our Miss Americas found mentors and allies that provided advice and encouragement later in life as well.

Donna Axum (1964) believed that she could not have accomplished all that she has without the guidance of others. "Through the years, I've had various people at different junctions in my life who have been influential in my growth and development. A choir director in Eldorado, Arkansas, had a great impact on my vocal development, expression on stage and the way I interpreted and enjoyed music. Other mentors at the University of Texas when I was working there gave me guidance and encouragement at a time in my life when I really needed it."

Apprentice yourself to a master. They have already forged a path toward their dream and can show you the way toward yours.

Success leaves footprints

People who have accomplished what you yearn to do provide you with a concrete example that it can be done. Role models inspire us by what they have had to overcome to accomplish their seemingly impossible goals. Gurus, guides and allies can also be role models. You can find them close to home, written up in magazines and in the annals of history.

When Ericka Dunlap (2004) found out about Debbye Turner, Miss America 1990, she was encouraged to create a higher vision of herself. Debbye is an African-American woman, just like Ericka. "Everything about her spoke to me. If she could do it, well, then so could I!"

Debbye was Ericka's idol. "I'll never forget when I first met her when I was twenty years old. Tara Holland [1997] introduced me to her. I was excited about meeting Tara, but this was Debbye Turner. She set the precedent for me. After Tara introduced me, Debbye said, 'Hi Ericka,' and I started bawling. I had all these jitters because I never thought I would meet her. She took her powder sponge out of her compact and dabbed at my face. That really sealed it. I was just stunned. She grabbed my arm and said 'Let's go talk.' That helped me to realize that becoming Miss America was attainable. I could impact lives just like she impacted mine."

Role models help us wipe the smudges from our glasses so we can see our way to the future more clearly. They exemplify a different way of being than we can imagine on our own. Then they motivate us to try just that bit harder by their very presence.

Shawntel Smith (1996) was inspired by Heather Whitestone who became Miss America the year before Shawntel. "I was newly crowned Miss Oklahoma. I found out that Heather Whitestone, the current Miss America, was going to be speaking in Tulsa. At that point I was planning to just do my best at the Miss America competition. I still felt that my being short and not your typical Miss America could be a barrier. I had my doubts that I could become Miss America, but after I heard Heather speak, I knew that I could do the job. That inspired me to push a little harder, reach a little higher, work on my song and go to the gym one more time, to condition myself to be the best I could be. I wanted to make Oklahoma proud."

Role models prove that most limits are self-imposed and that great things can be achieved. Their example can power your hope. Every person you meet may have a lesson for you. Ask them about it.

People like to say yes

Do you wonder why no one has shown up at your door just yet? If you carry your dream around like a limp dishrag instead of a regal banner, you'll never find out. Success requires influencing others to help you. You never know who might be willing. The most amazing thing happens when you share your passion and ask – people say yes.

Look around. Are there people who can help you get closer to your dream? If so, there are a few things you need to do to get them on your side.

First, you have to do your homework to learn more about these people and the subject at hand. They need to see that you are serious about your pursuit. Wait until your instincts (not your fear) tell you that the time is right. Your preparation and thoughtfulness demonstrate seriousness of purpose and will bolster your credibility. Come prepared and you will find gurus open and more than willing. Ask and yes, you shall receive.

Jennifer Berry (2006) found that it made a big difference when she reached outside of her inner circle to get help. She knew that getting to the next level would require more than she could do on her own. "We women try and do everything ourselves. I had to admit that I needed help. Then I was able to reach out to people who were professionals and ask them to help me become my very best. That was a turning point for me."

Many people find it difficult to ask for help. Some of us don't believe that we deserve it. Others, who grew up in homes that valued independence and self-sufficiency view asking for help as an admission of weakness. So we try and do it all ourselves. For others the fear of rejection holds them back. When you ask, you discover that people don't think any less of you and, in fact, are enthusiastic about helping you achieve your goals. What a relief not to have to pretend to know it all!

"I was always pretty good at asking for help," said Susan Powell (1981). "But a lot of people will not. That's huge. Five people, my inner circle, were my angels. I could go to them and say I feel horrible about something. I need you to tell me honestly what you think. I made it a point to surround myself with people who I trusted. I was so lucky to have people who loved me and were willing to tell me the truth. I hope that I can do that for someone, someday."

If you wait for your guru to come to you, you'll be standing in the wings for a long time. You must take the initiative and approach the individual who you think would make a good mentor. Sometimes they will appear, but it is up to you to turn them into a Yoda who will guide, instruct and protect you.

Identifying your Yoda

The people who can help don't walk around wearing a sash that identifies them as future mentors. A mentor can appear in many forms – a neighbor, a beloved aunt, a colleague at work, a stranger who serendipity puts in your path at just the right time.

It helps to follow your instincts and identify people who intrigue and inspire you. When you have an emotional connection with someone and trust them, she – or he – can help you push past your limits.

To find them Rebecca King (1974) would counsel you to look for someone with whom you connect. So many of us hate to make that first move, but she says, "You need to go over and say hello. Then a door may open to a relationship with someone you really enjoy being with and talking to and who appreciates you."

Don't underestimate the role of chemistry. We've all met people that we've felt an immediate attraction to because of their personalities, their warmth, their knowledge, their position. Your Yoda's values and emotional style should mesh with yours. You are going to be relying on this individual for advice and inspiration that will affect every aspect of your life. This will be a partnership and should feel like one. They should believe in what you are trying to achieve, otherwise their advice will be hollow.

Rebecca concurs. "Your antenna needs to be up. Your gut will tell you if this is somebody that you enjoy talking to. A mentor is not going to come up to you and say, 'Hey, I want to be your mentor.' You have to make a conscious effort. I don't think there is necessarily one mentor for all your life. You would be extraordinarily lucky if you had a family member or friend that was exceptional."

You can consider star power when you are assessing potential mentors. People in high places may be able to open doors to opportunities you wouldn't be able to get on your own. They already have credibility with their contacts; and if they make an introduction, others will pay attention. Though this may seem manipulative, if you are clear with them and yourself about your expectations, it won't be.

If a potential mentor doesn't know you or isn't convinced of the validity of your dreams, it's unlikely that she will say yes. So try to develop some kind of relationship before you ask. No one wants to make an upfront commitment without knowing what it entails.

It is perfectly acceptable to call someone you may not know, explain who you are and ask if they would be willing to meet with you informally. Most people who have been successful, when approached with respect, are more than willing to give back by helping someone else. I know. I've done it myself – both as the mentor and the mentee.

You can also put together a small group of people that you admire and respect. You become each other's board of directors. Meet regularly and before you know it, you will all have achieved more than you ever could on your own.

Sometimes it seems like fate puts someone in your path at just the right time. If you keep your eyes, ears and heart open, a guide may magically appear with just the right mix of skills and personality.

In addition, old-style mentoring by one person can be augmented by a broad array of mentoring options. Not only those gurus, guides and allies we meet in person, but the internet, books and other media contain useful information from experts you haven't met. Teleseminars, chat rooms, networking groups, and professional associations also hold the possibility of providing solutions and support.

If the first people you identify can't or won't help you, keep looking. The world is strewn with gems. Sometimes you have to look around not only the corner but the block to find your diamond.

Accepting Yoda's help

Gurus and guides remember a time when they were in your shoes, when they needed help at some point in their journey and the expertise of someone who had been there. The best of them will be empathetic with your reasonable fears and concerns. At the same time, they want to feel that the hours they have been with you have been spent wisely. The unwritten contract between the two of you implies that you agree to heed much of their advice and work to change. Sometimes you will have to do what may be difficult for you. If you are unwilling to implement what they advise, then you're wasting your guru's time – and your own.

Gretchen Carlson (1989) cautions, "Do not automatically trust the experts." Just because someone is an expert, it doesn't mean that person will always have the solution that is right for you. There is *always* more than one right answer. It helps to understand both their reasons for and your response to their recommendations. At the same time that you respect and accept what others suggest, you have to check it against your own internal compass. If it doesn't feel right, it may not be right for you. Sometimes the timing may be wrong. Then again, be aware that the reluctance you may feel may be based on fear – fear of failure, fear of rejection, even fear of success.

Lee Meriwether (1955) learned a hard but important lesson from her guru that has helped form the basis of her believability as an actor through the next five decades. "My high school drama teacher, a fabulous woman, didn't give lectures. Her lessons were stories. One day we were talking about what you say to someone after a performance when they weren't very good. She was teaching us proper backstage etiquette. She said that you can compliment the author or the playwright. You skirt the person's performance and tell them the play or the playwright was wonderful and that you enjoyed it so much. Then you are still being truthful to yourself and not saying anything hurtful to them. Actors are in a fragile state having just come off the stage."

By asking for the truth, hard as it was, Lee grew as an actor. "I was in a play in college and my high school drama teacher came to see me. I was so excited that she made the trip. Afterwards she came backstage and said to me, 'Oh Lee, this is such a wonderful play.' I started crying. Then she realized what she had done. I asked her to tell me what she really thought. She asked me if I wanted her to be honest and I said yes, please. I didn't know that I was pushing and overacting. I thought that people couldn't tell what I felt. She told me, 'When you feel it, you don't have to show people. They will see.' So many times through the years that has come back. I remind myself that the audience will see it if you feel it."

Shawntel Smith (1996) learned a similar lesson about heeding advice. "I remember a discussion with Rick Brinkley, head of the Miss Oklahoma pageant. We were at the Polo Grill in Tulsa. He took me to a public place because he knew we were going to have a serious talk. He thought I would handle it better if we were someplace public. He told me that he could see me as Miss America, but that I had to see myself as Miss America too. He would work with me however I chose, whether it was doing enough to have a good showing or doing enough to become Miss America. That day was emotional for me. I cried because he believed in me that much. He was willing to put everything on the line to help me become my best. He pushed me and made me visually picture myself with the crown being placed on my head. That was definitely a turning point."

Your guru will be invaluable to your success. If there is any way you can reciprocate the favor, do. Maybe there will be nothing that you can do for your Yoda except to express your appreciation for her help. Celebrate your success together. She will welcome knowing when you achieve your dream and later that you have followed in her generous footsteps and helped others. That will be a great reward indeed.

At some point your relationship will change. As the level of advice you need diminishes and you move from disciple to colleague, the time may come to renegotiate the terms of your relationship. It can turn into a friendship, or retreat to being respected and admired acquaintances. It may happen through deliberate discussion or by the natural progression of the relationship. Only the two of you can decide. Then it may be time for a new mentor or none at all. For now. Until your next big adventure into the unknown.

This relationship will change your life. Use it well. Reward the efforts of your mentor by becoming the woman of your own dreams. She will love you for it.

Allies are your home-team fans

Enroll every voice you can in your vision. They will be your back-up singers. Successful people cultivate positive, supportive relationships that cheer them on and help them weather rejections and self-doubts.

Several of the Formers credit their mothers with bucking them up when the weight of responsibility cloaking their shoulders as Miss America became overwhelming.

The morning following her crowning, Shawntel Smith (1996) was reorganizing her suitcase on the bathroom floor of her hotel suite, deciding what to take to New York and what to send home to Oklahoma. "All of a sudden I started crying," she said. "I was overwhelmed with winning the title, but most of all I was concerned about my ability to do this job. The tears started pouring down my face. I didn't even have to tell my mother. She knew what I was going through at that moment. I'll never forget what she did. She lifted my chin and said, 'Shawntel, I believe in you. You will be a great Miss America.' That was all I needed at that moment. From that point on, I knew that I was on a mission."

Every bit of encouragement helps. Just before Deidre Downs (2005) left for the pageant, her voice coach, who was also on the board of Miss Alabama, told her a story. "Her coach said, 'I remember talking to a Miss Alabama in the early nineties. She went to Atlantic City and had fun, but she didn't think that she could be Miss America. So she didn't really give it her best. She came back and regretted it. Looking back, she thought she could have done better. Maybe she could have won if she put her heart into it. Who knows?' Then she said to me, 'Don't go into it thinking you can't be Miss America. Go up there and believe in yourself and go all out.' That helped me refocus."

The people who help and support you sometimes believe in you when you don't believe in yourself. Their encouragement can help you deal with the self-doubts that assail you.

Tawny Godin (1976) was fortunate to find allies at every stage of her life who were willing to take a risk with her because they saw her potential. Without their support she never would have survived as a young woman in the competitive world of television news reporting. "One of my main anchors at NBC saw what a difficult time I was having and always said, 'You can do this. If you need any help, come to me.' A lot of people encouraged me that way. You have to believe in yourself and connect with the people who believe in you too."

Few people reach their dreams alone. Encouragement can come from the most unexpected places. Heather Whitestone (1995) told me a story about a guy named Bob. The year before she won she went to the national pageant to see what it was like. "He had been selling Miss America programs on the boardwalk for years. I came by his stand to buy one. He looked at me and said, 'You come back next year and you will be Miss America.' I looked at him and thought – is he crazy? He had no idea I was deaf. When I came back the following year to compete, I didn't think he would remember me, but he did, and he remembered exactly what he had said. That inspired me."

As a girl from Brandon, Mississippi in 1957, Mary Ann Mobley (1959) was not schooled in the sophisticated ways of big city productions. Luckily the kindness of strangers made all the difference. "I still think of my becoming Miss America as a Cinderella story. I always wanted to do musicals and I didn't know how I was going to be able to do that. I had come from a sheltered environment. My father had been very strict, with rules and regulations I had to follow.

"I went to the Pageant without an orchestration for my song. I gave the conductor one sheet of music. He asked me if that was all of it. To his credit, when I said yes, he didn't fall on the floor laughing. He tapped his baton on his podium and said, 'Ladies and gentlemen of the orchestra, we have a young lady here that needs our help. If you recognize a note, write it in.'

"The night I was to do my talent I was panicked. I had never been on a stage like that or sung with an orchestra. Backstage two stagehands were holding the curtain for me to go out. One of them patted me on the shoulder and said, 'Go get 'em, Mississippi.' He gave me that little extra encouragement that I needed. I knew I couldn't run off the stage. I would have embarrassed the whole state of Mississippi. I wish I could go back and thank him."

People who are dissatisfied with their lives and who choose to stay stuck will not want you to succeed. They should not be part of your inner circle. If you've got any people like that in your life, you need to divest yourself of their company if at all possible. If you can't, because they are related to you or tied to you in some unbreakable way, then you've got to find a way to dilute their negative impact.

Vonda Van Dyke (1965) believes that she always has a choice in how to react to the events and people in her life. "There are positive people and there are negative people. I don't usually keep myself around negative people. I like to surround myself with positive people. If I am involved in a friendship and it becomes negative, if I see them discouraging other people or me, I'll leave that friendship. It's a matter of focus. I refuse to be dragged down by somebody else."

Just like your gurus, the greatest gift of appreciation you can give your allies is to fulfill your potential. Then they know that their faith in you was justified.

Pay it forward

It was an eye-opening moment for many of the young women who became Miss America when they realized that they now had a forum, as Tara Holland (1997) put it, "to speak something into others' lives" that would have a positive impact.

Shawntel Smith (1996) exemplified this idea. "I was on a mission to share how important education was to young people across this nation. Maybe I could help inspire and motivate someone to go to the next level. Then they could become the person that they had hidden in their heart."

In retrospect Rebecca King (1974) always wished she had had mentors. Now she makes sure to mentor other young women. "It short-circuits so much. It's empowering to know that it is possible to accomplish this goal out in a mystical land when you're twenty-one or forty-one. And that getting there is not necessarily a direct path."

Rebecca values the role she plays these days as a guide to younger people. "You're there to help people in their lives and use your experience, your knowledge and your understanding." She sees her legal practice as an opportunity to mentor and guide as well. "I want to help youth set a standard of success in their life and also impact their parents' lives and get them involved. I can be talking to them one-on-one and they will say, "Mrs. Dreman [Rebecca's married name], I can't do that." I tell them that I'm not willing to accept that. You have to give yourself a chance and try a little harder. I'm not giving up on you yet. I don't want you to say, 'I can't.' I want you to say 'I can.' You know you can do this."

She tells them that she believes in them. "I'm not asking you to do something that I think you can't accomplish. And if you're starting from a zero knowledge base and you even get to a two out of ten, it's more than what you had before. At least you can say you experienced it. Rarely do I see the kids walk away from something without gaining at least some greater self-knowledge and confidence."

Though our Miss Americas aren't princesses who need a knight to rescue them, they welcome the appearance of a fairy godmother or a Yoda who can show them the way. So when you undertake your hero's journey and give yourself fully to the adventure, know that you will not be alone. Your gurus, guides and allies will appear by your side and hand you off into your future. Just like Yoda, they will say, "Strong enough alone, you are not. Help you I will, yes."

LESSON 11:
The Act-as-if Princple

"Act the way you'd like to be and soon you'll be the way you act." Dr. George Crane, syndicated newspaper columnist

Many successful people aren't as confident as they appear. High achievers often "wing it," hiding their insecurities behind their audacity.

As you expand your self-image and vision for the future, you may experience moments when your discomfort is at a fever pitch. Don the mantle of your desired self and behave as your dreams demand. Act confident and you will be confident. Act fearless and fear will subside. Act like a leader and people will follow. This is the act-as-if principle.

"My mom always taught me to act-as-if," said Angie Baraquio (2001). "When I went onstage, people would look at me like I was some kind of expert; I was no expert!" It wasn't until she competed for the crown in 2000 that she fully understood the power of the act-as-if principle. "I discovered that when I acted-as-if, I was confident. I acted-as-if I knew what I was talking about. I acted-as-if I belonged on that stage as Miss America. I competed twice before at Miss Hawaii and hadn't won. This time I carried myself all the way through as I thought Miss America would."

Quaking knees

Several of the Formers confessed to panic attacks every time they had to perform or speak in public. Self-doubts about being good enough, smart enough, even pretty enough have plagued many of these beautiful women throughout their lives. By employing the act-as-if principle, they were able to step beyond the boundaries of those limiting beliefs.

"I love the concept of act-as-if," said Marilyn Van Derbur (1958). "I've done that most of my life. I didn't think I could make it down that runway, so I walked 'as-if.' I walked up to the podium as if I was confident. You would never have known that I thought I was dying. So when I acted-as-if that confidence was true, it eventually became a part of me."

Marilyn learned to act-as-if early in her life. To the outside world, she was the perfect child, though her nights were filled with the terror and pain of the incest committed by her father. In spite of the horror of her upbringing, she managed to use the skills she had learned acting-as-if to her advantage later in life by becoming a renowned motivational speaker and advocate for victims of sexual abuse.

An accomplished singer, actress and television host, Susan Powell (1981) has to cloak herself in confidence every time she goes for an audition. Not only does she have to act for the camera, but she has to act as if she's the right person for the role. "Every time I audition it's as if it's for the first time," she said.

When you act as if you are as smart, beautiful, outgoing, competent, talented, and deserving as you wish to be, others believe you, even if you may not fully believe in yourself. They have no reason not to take you at face value. Your actions reinforce your beliefs and over time you become the competent person you wish to be. There is power in pretending when it's in the service of a higher goal.

Make no mistake. To be plausible, you have to work at acquiring the substance to bolster the image. Each of our Miss Americas put out significant effort to become the women they are today. One day they realized that they weren't just acting as if they are Miss America. They *were* Miss America.

The crown, the cape and the sword

As a natural part of growing up, every single one of us, at one time or another, pretended to be someone or something else. Often that someone was a higher vision of our self – a princess when we donned a jeweled crown, a dragon slayer when we brandished a glittering sword or a caped superhero who would save the world.

Pretend play is a way for children to make sense of the world, process new experiences and try on different roles and emotions. To act as-if involves role-playing and improvisation. When a child dons her crown and commands others to do her bidding, she is learning about leadership. When she rescues the poor fellow from the claws of the dragon, she is learning about bravery in the service of others. When she explores dark and scary caves in search of treasure, she learns to confront her fears. When she plots her way through unknown territory, she learns problem-solving skills. When the heroine crosses bottomless chasms in a single leap, she learns to trust her instincts and take risks.

"I was very girly," said Ericka Dunlap (2004), one of the very small number of Miss Americas who participated in the child pageant system. "When I was six years old, my mom told me about American Coed. My mom had me in tap, ballet and jazz. She asked me if this was something I would be interested in and gave me all the paperwork. I was so excited to see the little girls on the front of the pamphlet. They had crowns on and wore the big-girl glittery dresses with all the rhinestones and beads. I had three older sisters who had conditioned me. I loved painting my nails, doing my hair, putting on vast amounts of lip gloss. I would go to sleep every night with that pamphlet in my hand."

When children adopt the role of a powerful character, they feel in control, which enhances their self-identity. The stakes are low in this pretend world and the child is the authority. She can decide at any moment what the outcome will be and adjust her behavior to fit the circumstances. By pretending to be someone else, to have other powers and behave in novel ways, she makes sense of events and transforms the world to meet her needs. It is a powerful force, this acting-as-if. It takes possibility and turns it into reality, even if only for a moment.

Heather Whitestone (1995) will tell you how when she was a child she loved to dress up in a sparkly crown and cape and parade around the house. She loved anything that had to do with royalty. Princess Diana was her role model. Starting in her teens, Heather's passion gave her the courage, in spite of her deafness, to compete. As Heather and Ericka grew up, pageants became a way for them to play out their childhood fantasies.

As adults, most of us still get a kick out of adopting a different identity at a costume party. I once held a Halloween party where the invitation said to come as you *really* are. One woman wore her corporate suit on one half her body and a slinky, femme fatale dress on the other. She was Mistress of the Universe by day, irresistibly female by night.

The act-as-if principle is used in the adult learning environment, such as workshops and seminars. Role-playing and mastering pretend situations are time-honored techniques to test and acquire new behaviors and skills.

So why are we so hesitant to role-play our most successful self in our grown-up lives? Why can't we take the act-as-if skills we learned as children and use them to our advantage as adults?

We used props as kids – towel capes to help us fly, wooden swords to slay dragons, and magic wands to make our wishes come true. Why not take what props you need – a smile for confidence, a grab-your-fear-by-the-neck attitude, an intrepid willingness to take a risk and be your own heroine?

Why it works

By acting as if you are the person you want to be, regardless of feeling incompetent or fraudulent, you become that person. That capable, assured woman is the woman that others see. Even how you dress and carry yourself makes a difference. If your clothes don't fit properly, are spotted or torn, or inappropriate for the place and time, people will see you as being inadequate and inept, even if you're not. If you convey an attitude of sullenness or apathy, even if it's a cover for shyness or fear, others won't want to be around you.

Dress and act worthy of respect, as if you are that successful executive, pageant winner, or champion, and people will treat you as if you already are.

During the three years after she was Miss America, Phyllis George (1971) appeared in commercials and co-hosted Candid Camera with Allen Funt and the Miss America Pageant with Bert Parks. CBS

Sports, seeing her potential, offered Phyllis a thirteen-week option as a sportscaster at a time when television sports was dominated by men.

"I could have said, 'But I can't do that. I don't know how.' Though I'd always been a sports fan, I was not an athlete or an expert. In fact, I had no professional experience in the sports world. Somehow in the middle of all these uncertainties, I decided to accept the offer, partly because I needed the job and partly because something inside told me I could do it. I had little evidence to support this instinct, but I knew it was worth a try." Phyllis showed that she could disarm a stubborn interview subject and convince him to reveal himself to a television audience. Her producers recognized a unique talent and signed her to a three-year deal, which ended up running ten years. Her ability to act-as-if paid big dividends.

Again, there is an important difference, of course, between just faking it and acting-as-if. When you fake a feeling or behavior, you are just going through the motions. You are nice to Aunt Edna because your mother wants you to be, or you become an accountant rather than an architect because your father wants your future to be secure. Underneath may be a hidden resentment or rebelliousness. It isn't the same energy as when you act-as-if for yourself, because then you are acting in the service of a higher goal that *you* desire. Your motivation and attitude come from a completely different place and the results of your efforts reflect that. Phyllis understood that.

When you model your ideal self, you develop a success mindset. At the very moment that you direct your inner vision and outer actions toward what you want to become, you set in motion the very energy that will get you there. You begin the process of transformation.

As Susan Powell (1981) understood, transformation starts from the inside out. "I just kept going back to visualizing myself in the role until I was comfortable seeing myself in it. I wasn't afraid. From my teachers and singing, I knew all about thinking ahead and visualization. It was powerful."

The farther something that you want to do is from your experience, understanding or knowledge, the louder the buzz of discomfort, the greater the dissonance. But you've got to start somewhere.

See in your mind's eye the woman you want to become. Imagine the feelings, talents and skills the person possesses; the way others respond to her and the situations she wants to be in. When you start to visualize and act in a way that supports your dreams, you start to rewire your circuits. The more you do it, the more these new perceptions become embedded in your character. This is the power of the act-as-if principle.

Living with dissonance

When we try something new and challenging, we often experience anxiety about our ability to succeed, ranging from a flush under our freckles to throat-closing terror. Because we have minimal experience to back up our claims of competence, we are assailed by self-doubt. But such feelings don't inhibit our Miss Americas. They know that when they act-as-if, there is a part of them that has already taken on that new identity. It may be very small, but it exists, and now they are auditioning it for others.

Angie Baraquio (2001) recognized that everything she had done in her life had given her the skills to manage her new role, even if it was outside of her comfort zone. "As the new Miss America, I was sitting with a media trainer before I was about to go on a thirteen-city tour. I had done some TV in the past and had hosted a show with my sisters before I won Miss Hawaii. The trainer said, 'Wow! You've already done this.' They said I was good to go. I felt really happy to know that I wasn't completely green when it came to interviewing and that my whole life had been gearing up for this moment."

An extreme version of the act-as-if principle is the imposter syndrome, which has been studied by psychologists for several decades. High-achieving women seem the most prone to experiencing it. They have a secret, shameful sense that they are not as capable as others think they are. Despite external proof of their competence, somehow they feel that they don't deserve what they have achieved and are frauds. They often believe that luck played a part or that they have deceived others. When such thinking persists over a lifetime, in spite of the reality of their achievements, their beliefs may start to border on the pathological.

These psychologists did find an upside to the discomfort and anxiety that can accompany a new role. Feelings of inadequacy can protect against subconscious delusions of grandeur. It's a delicate balancing act – knowing that you are good at what you do versus believing that you are superior to others. It can inject a note of realism into otherwise magical thinking.

A dash of the imposter syndrome can spice up the act-is-if principle and encourage you to try a little harder. A study by two Purdue University psychologists revealed that women who scored high on a questionnaire measuring anxiety, imposter feelings and approach to academic goals, also reported a strong desire to show that they could do better than others. They weren't afraid of competition and hard work.

Lots of well-adjusted people feel like a fraud, yet go on to achieve in spite of it. They use that emotion to push themselves to higher levels of achievement. Others are imposter imposters. They adopt self-deprecation as a strategy to gain sympathy and lower expectations. Others can sense when humility isn't genuine. It's one of those "you know it when you see it" kind of things. Check your motives and then your methods.

Teetering on the brink of adventure isn't always comfortable. When we act-as-if, we stand at the edge of a precipice. The secret to managing the dissonance is doing your homework and leaping with your whole heart. You can't cross a chasm in two bounds.

Evolution

Evolution is the process of making small incremental changes over time ultimately resulting in new species. When you practice a positive form of pretending, you are making changes to your psyche. When you proceed as if you've already reached your goals, you're almost there. When you behave as you wish to be perceived in all that you do, you act like the new creature of success that you will become.

To act-as-if, you must change your behavior. When you change your behavior, you are changing your attitude. When you change your behavior and your attitude, you change your thoughts. When you change your behavior, attitude and thoughts, you change the chemistry in your brain. When you change the chemistry in your brain, your metamorphosis is complete.

When our experience and success catch up with our self-image, our inner and outer selves merge and we no longer feel like an imposter in what we are doing. After all, it's experience that creates comfort. "Oh, I've been here before," some small voice pipes up inside. "Just maybe, I *do* know my way around." Our self-confidence blossoms. We suck in our tummies and stare down our fears. What a rush!

Marilyn Van Derbur (1958) understood that. "Eventually the person that you pretend to be becomes a part of you. I've always been good at that. I had to play a role or fall apart. It's the only way I could get through the pageants and later all the speaking engagements. It's a life-changing concept because you change how you think."

Those who use the fear of being unmasked as a fraud as a reason to not go after their dreams are playing it safe. Too safe. They exploit this excuse to stay stuck on the well-beaten path of their daily life.

In many situations, feeling fraudulent is a realistic response. Maybe you're new at your job, or one of a meager number making a mark in your profession. You may feel like you don't fit in and may very well be an outsider in that environment. You may aspire to accomplish something you don't quite know how to do. Give yourself permission to make mistakes. Everything takes practice. So don't take your self-doubt as a sign of ineptness. Recognize that it may be a normal response.

"Put on your make-up. Put on your clothes," said Susan Powell (1981). "Sometimes if I fix the outside a little bit, the inside starts to follow. I think that all of us women would say pretty much the same thing."

At the very heart of the act-as-if principle is courage. Moving through your terror of consequences is a brave and audacious act. The moment you leap from the precipice ignites a thrilling transformation. By the time you scramble to the other side, you have become a different person.

Many of the Miss Americas were panicked when they first had to speak in public. They walked through that fear, put some Vaseline on their teeth to hold their smiles, took a few deep breaths, and hoofed it to the podium. After a while, their fear of being found out started to subside and their thermostats returned to normal.

Every act of creation is first an act of disruption. Certainly, it would be easier if a step-by-step recipe for success existed. When you are afraid to be wrong, you cripple your ability to move forward. Allowing yourself to fail as you try out new behaviors is the only way to grow into that new person. Though it may seem a paradox, this sense of inadequacy can fuel a desire to excel. It can help you get unstuck. It doesn't mean that you are being dishonest. You are pulling out the best of who you are in the process of acting-as-if. When you look back a year from now, the creature you see will be a mere shadow of the woman you have become. Evolution is real.

Mind meld

The power is within you. In spite of the internal gremlins that mock your desires for greatness, another part of your spirit knows that you are capable and harbors the courage for you to risk change.

And let's face it, lots of people don't see beneath the surface. So if you walk, talk and act your greatness with some small spark of self-belief fueling your actions, others see it. Otherwise they wouldn't believe, encourage and support you. Deidre Downs (2005) says that others often see more in you than you do in yourself.

Donna Axum (1964), who has coached many pageant contestants, tells them, "If you want to be Miss America, you have to think like Miss America, carry yourself like Miss America and walk the walk like Miss America."

Donna would have considered Tara Holland (1997) a good student. Tara decided that in her fifth year of competing she would conduct herself as she believed Miss America would. "I needed to focus, so I made up two signs. I still have them. They were on yellow legal paper. I used a great big red permanent marker and wrote on them 'Be Miss America.' I put one on the bathroom mirror and the other on the vanity mirror so I would see them everyday. I wanted to remind myself to conduct myself as if I were Miss America.

"I studied the winners and read everything I could get my hands on," she continued. "In my mind Miss America was gracious. She was concerned about other people. She was considerate and kind. She put herself together well. She had her focus right. She was success-minded. She didn't act like a lot of people do when they are twenty-three years old. She was not self-consumed, although she took good care of herself. So I kept reminding myself, 'When you leave here and go to the gym or are in professional situations, be Miss America.' I was training my mind. I saw myself in the role. I saw myself not just winning but living out the title. I saw myself in every facet of daily life as Miss America. I kept that image in front of me all the time."

Many of our Miss Americas who are performers understand how to act-as-if. On stage they can be whoever they want.

"When I'm on stage, I'm a different person," says Ericka Dunlap (2004). "Since childhood I felt this electricity that lit up my personality. In my everyday life I was a nerdy kid. I liked being in the books. I used to read the dictionary in the first and second grade. I was rather quiet, but I developed leadership skills through being in pageants and tapping into that other personality that I let out on stage." Ericka discovered that when she participated in pageants, she had to act like the woman she eventually became, exhibiting leadership, poise and confidence. "It was through those experiences that I was able to become the woman that I am now."

Eventually your feelings will catch up with reality. There will come a time when you are comfortable once again in your skin. Don't rest on your laurels. If you continue to challenge yourself, you'll be back in that intoxicating tempest of transformation again and again.

The next time, you'll be ready.

In all things, be smart

It goes without saying, there is no acting as-if when you are in a position to be responsible for others' lives. In those circumstances, whether you are an airline pilot, a physician, a teacher, a lawyer or a policeman, you've got to have the credentials and knowledge to actually do the job or admit when you don't. It's a huge responsibility.

Yet the act-as-if principle can also operate for those who have actually done the hard work and gotten their certificates of achievement. The first time a new lawyer argues her case before the jury, the fresh-out-of-school physician cares for a sick child or a newly minted teacher watches her students enter the classroom, they may be acting-as-if. Their sense of competency and confidence fluctuates as their new behaviors become part of their cells.

Even though that lawyer's heart may be pounding as she paces in front of the jury for the first time, even though a policewoman's hands may be shaking when she pats down a suspect, even when a pilot has butterflies that fly along with her at take off and landing, each one of them knows, deep down inside, that she can do the job. They've studied and trained. They're ready.

In the movie *Working Girl*, Melanie Griffith plays a secretary working for a venture capital firm who assumes her boss's identity after her female boss is laid up with a broken leg. To the outside world, Melanie *is* the boss. Dressed in her employer's expensive clothing, she pulls off a huge deal because she acts-as-if she is a high powered, in-the-know executive. Even Hollywood recognized that to be plausible, Melanie's character had to know her stuff, do her research and find a way to set herself apart in the world of high finance. She worked harder and smarter than the other "girls" in the secretarial pool.

You can't expect to become a new you without discomfort. Take a deep breath and get out there. Be the person you aspire to be. The act-as-if principle pushes you out of your familiarity zone and into the unknown.

The good news is that the boundaries of the comfort zone are movable. The more you act-as-if, the more aligned your inner and outer self will feel. You have to trust in the drive that compels you to act like the person you want to be.

Rather than give in to those feelings of inadequacy, remind yourself that everyone who has any modicum of self-awareness and doesn't harbor grandiose illusions about themselves, experiences such feelings. So many of the Formers talked about feeling inadequate, but they put themselves out there anyway. A time came when the two halves of their mind and heart came together and they were one.

As Marilyn Van Derbur (1958) says, "You just do it." Like Phyllis and Tara, Angie and Ericka, all of the Miss Americas I spoke to, in spite of their discomfort, their fear of looking foolish, their terror of being "found out," accepted the challenge. They lived with stretched and sore muscles from pushing themselves until they evolved into that fabulous woman they saw in their mind's eye.

How badly do you yearn to be your own Miss America? If you want it badly enough, then you'll start acting as that woman. Practice when no one else is looking. The extraordinary you does exist. You just haven't been willing to show it to the world.

LESSON 12:
Once Is Never Enough

"Nobody can go back and start a new beginning, but anyone can start today and make a new ending." Maria Robinson, author

The moment she is crowned, Miss America becomes the sweetheart of the nation. But when the spotlight moves on after three hundred and sixty-five days, she is challenged to shape the rest of her life. These beautiful women have discovered that whether they are twenty-seven or fifty-seven, they can choose to change direction. The arc of their lives proves that opportunities for personal enrichment, professional achievement and public philanthropy abound at every age. It's the final lesson they teach us.

Shawntel Smith (1996) said, "During my year I was used to being picked up in a limo, surrounded by security, flying from one destination to the next and being treated like royalty. The world views you on a pedestal. But when I gave up that crown, I had a decision to make. What did I want to do with the rest of my life? It's like hitting the reset button.

"Did I want to continue to speak and use my role as Miss America to promote myself? Or did I want to do something completely different? I decided I wanted to be on the speaking circuit. My mother was my manager and helped drive the business; she was just amazing. I did it for seven years until I got married. Then my husband and I started our own technology business and I became a mom. I still work in the business today. I'm in control of my own destiny.

"Most of the women who are crowned Miss America are very strong," Shawntel continued. "They're ambitious women, women with philosophies and ideas about what they want to do with their lives and who they want to impact. We examine what is before us and then pave a new way for ourselves."

Rebecca King (1974) shares her lesson. "If you think that your life has ended at twenty-three when you've accomplished all of your goals as Miss America, that's a sad story. You have many years ahead of you. I still have lots of pages to turn in my book, more chapters still to be written.

"I'm looking forward to whatever will happen next. Do I need to make a plan? Absolutely. It doesn't matter how old I am. I have a bigger picture for myself of working in a larger arena to solve issues that have an impact on society, like transportation, the environment, social services or health care. I want to go into an organization and use my leadership and communication skills for positive change. It's a transitional time for me. My kids are grown. I'm pondering what I'm going to do next."

Throughout her life, work and family have required Donna Axum (1964) to relocate. Her approach to changes has always turned them into a positive experience. "Bloom where you're planted is another one of my philosophies. You find a church community, join your alumni group, get involved in community organizations and you've got automatic friends. That's what I did. Rather than just sit there and do nothing, I got involved in my community to feel part of it. My fundamental belief is that part of our stewardship as human beings is to be of service to other people. For me it's been in education and the arts."

Lynda Meade (1960), who went to Parsons School of Design in New York City after her reign as Miss America, started an interior design business specializing in French antiques when she was forty-eight. Now she has her own shop and several designers working for her. "I would like to work until I'm at least seventy. Then I would like my antiques shop to keep going without me." When I asked what she learned about herself over the years, she said, "I don't want to sound self-deprecating, but there are so many people with enormous gifts and talent. I think that I don't have any great gifts like that. But I have the gift of being really healthy and stable. I know myself. I know I'm only happy when I'm active."

She went on to share with me how she came to start her business. Once her children were almost on their own she became restless and cast about for something to keep her occupied. "I had only one unhappy period in my life, when my children were pretty well raised and I hadn't started my business yet. I did a lot of civic and charitable work. I helped start a woman's organization that helps deaf children. I played a lot of tennis and we traveled a lot. But it wasn't enough. I needed to work. I had gone a lot of years without doing anything professionally. It was a bit hard for me to make that leap into a professional life. I wanted to go into interior design, but I was a little afraid to just hang out my shingle. The Miss America experience taught me that, if winning can happen to anybody as unprepared as I was, then I could do anything."

The legacy they leave

Each generation of Miss Americas has been outspoken about issues that matter to them. In 1989 the Miss America Organization, recognizing the causes that previous Miss Americas supported and the influence that being Miss America can have on promoting important issues, formalized the requirement for a community service platform. Throughout their lives, our Miss Americas have taken on the daunting task of advocating for such causes as literacy, higher education, AIDs awareness and prevention, tolerance for diversity, values in education, drunk driving prevention, veterans' rights, internet awareness, pediatric cancer, Alzheimer's, arts in education, and the plight of children in Appalachia and third world countries among a myriad of others. They have been appointed to Presidential commissions, influenced Congress and lobbied state and local legislatures. They have comforted children and soldiers in hospitals and motivated students in schools. They have sat on the boards of worthwhile organizations, advocated for the less fortunate and promoted activism. They have raised funds to support causes important to them. In the process they have inspired millions of people over the years and won numerous awards. All of these important efforts have occurred while they raise their families and lead professional lives.

Tara Holland (1997) recounts the story of the time she was invited to lunch in Kennebunkport, Maine at the home of George and Barbara Bush. "You can't go through that year without being changed, because of the people you meet and the experiences you have. Most people, even if they die at eighty-five, won't experience what I was fortunate to experience. I sat down with the President of the United States and talked over important issues. I sat with the First Lady, Barbara Bush, and she said to me 'How can we work together on literacy and what can we get done?' " The crown provided the microphone for Tara, as it has for all of our Miss Americas, to speak about issues they passionately believe in, not only during their reign but also for the rest of their lives.

The lessons they learned

Even the most wished-for experience can have unintended consequences. For many of the Formers the crown brought with it not only scholarship money and exposure, but also a huge responsibility and intense scrutiny of their flaws and missteps. It did not always yield the happiness-ever-after that they may have expected. Their lives were changed in ways both rewarding and difficult that they could never have anticipated.

They all learned that being Miss America is completely different from trying to become Miss America. Nicole Johnson (1999) talks about her year. "I learned what loneliness felt like and I hadn't known that before. I had been plucked out of my life and taken away from my friends and family. You're arguably somewhat famous and yet you're very alone and isolated, even though you're surrounded by so many people. I had been independent for a long time and it was hard to be dependent, travel with a traveling companion, and have people watching what I did. I'd never done anything wrong in my whole life and people were picking me apart."

Gretchen Carlson (1989) also faced many challenges she didn't expect. "The night I won, I looked at myself in the mirror and wondered what I had gotten myself into. I had not thought through what would happen. I don't know if you can even plan for that. I had only focused on trying to attain the position. It's one of those experiences that you have to live through to be able to explain. Some of what it took to win, like my talent, the violin, I wouldn't need during my year. The preparation for the position was so different than actually being in it. I learned that I don't always wake up on the right side of the bed, but when you are Miss America you have to. It was the toughest job I will ever have.

"The flip side is that it was the most wonderful experience. Even though I say that it was my toughest job, it was also the most rewarding because of the fabulous people I met. It teaches you communication skills that nobody could ever teach you. It's like a crash course on how to communicate for the rest of your life – speaking skills, getting up in front of people and giving speeches without much preparation at all. During my very first week, I was in Atlanta at a dinner with a thousand people. The gentleman in charge came and tapped me on the shoulder after the main course and told me that he was giving me a five-minute warning for my keynote. I had no idea that I was supposed to speak. I went to the bathroom, shaking, with a pad of paper and did a couple of bullet points. There were a lot of those kinds of experiences. How many twenty-two year olds are put in that kind of situation?"

As Gretchen noted, the experience of being Miss America has benefits that accrue over the years. She was able to take her communications skills and turn them into a successful career as a television news reporter and news show co-host.

As Angie Baraquio (2001) and other Formers told me, the title of Miss America, like no other opportunity for a young woman, sat them beside people they never would have met and unlocked doors they didn't know existed. "It's more empowering than you could ever imagine," said Angie. "People who said they were feminists believed that the Pageant put women down. On the contrary, it's the most empowering thing I've ever done in my whole life. You tell me what other position would allow you to meet the President of the United States, senators and congressmen, CEOs, celebrities and people of influence at such a young age."

What will it feel like as the years go by if you look back on adventures you wish you had gone on, risks you wish you had taken, people you wish you had met? How would your life have been different? We have all felt the sting of regret at one point or another. To counteract regret, say yes to yourself. Don't die wondering what you could have accomplished if only you had acted today.

When Angie decided to enter her first pageant at eighteen, she got the jitters. "I was a scholar-athlete. When I started doing the pageant thing it was very scary for me. The last year I competed, I talked to my sister who is ten years older. She said, 'Will you be able to look back when you are forty years old and say you don't regret not participating? If you can say that, then don't do it. But if you think you will regret it, you have to go for it.' I realized then that I would definitely regret it if I didn't go for it."

Heather French (2000) found the strength in her father's words to ensure that she didn't have any regrets. After competing for five years and each year coming up short of the crown, she felt that she couldn't do it any more. In her last year of eligibility, she lost the first local pageant she entered. "I was teaching, working two other jobs and going to school. I didn't think I could do all that was required to compete again. My mom, who is so wise, suggested that I put my decision on the back burner.

"My father was very ill in the hospital with strep pneumonia. The last thing he said to me before he slipped into a coma, from which he did recover, was that he wanted me to try one more time, that our veterans needed a Miss America. Up to that point, my dad had not been comfortable with me talking about his prescription drug addiction and his traumatic experiences in Vietnam. This was the first time I was allowed to tell his full story.

"It took my father almost dying to wake me up. So when I went to Miss America I had crossed all the 't's and dotted all the 'i's. I had been preparing myself for this huge goal that I had always dreamed of attaining. I wanted to make sure that, when I got to Atlantic City, I had no regrets. Even if I walked away without the crown, I would be proud of who I had become."

Life is too short not to do what you love. Donna Axum (1964) says, "I want to have lots of celebrations of accomplishments throughout my life instead of regrets."

When we are young, we ask ourselves what we want to be when we grow up. Most of us never stop asking that question and over the years, the answer can change. Like our Miss Americas, at every age, you can straighten your crown, look the next challenge in the eye and know that nothing can stop you. Then you won't have any regrets. You learned that lesson well.

The sisterhood

Each of our Miss Americas feels the mantle of history and tradition and makes choices in her life to honor that responsibility. "So many women who came before us made the Pageant what is today. To me the legacy is huge," continued Angie. "I remember being in Atlantic City and seeing all the former Miss Americas' gowns and their pictures and the winning moments scrolling on the TV, over and over. I thought, 'I want my face to be up there one day.' You could feel the presence of all the women who have appeared in that convention hall before twenty-five thousand people. The hall must encompass so many stories, so many women's dreams. I am honored to be part of that huge legacy.

"When my year was over, I just wanted to take who I am and return to a normal life. Yet people will always call you Miss America. Phyllis George told me 'I don't care if you become the president of the United States. I don't care if you walk on the moon. People will always refer to you as a former Miss America. It's a part of who you are now and forever.'"

Jennifer Berry (2006) discovered the support system that exists when she was inducted into that close-knit sisterhood. "Being Miss America is so different from being a former Miss America. You go through your year, the hard work, the exhaustion. It's a crazy year where you become a completely different person. You have the foundation of who you are, but you change and grow so much. The night you crown your successor you go to your first Formers' party. That is your introduction to being a former Miss America. All of them came up to me and said that they were so happy that I was part of them now. Being one of eighty-five women in the world who have been in that position and shared the same experiences is so special. The night you give up your crown nothing has to be said. Everyone understands."

Wanting to give back to the Pageant that changed her life, Heather French (2000) pays it forward by mentoring contestants and new Miss

Americas. "A lot of us come back every year to the Pageant because we feel the weight of responsibility to offer guidance to future generations and to pass on the traditions. I've taken it on myself to be the person who calls my new Miss America sister to help her understand what to expect during her year and to encourage her to think about the transition she will experience after the spotlight moves on."

Shawntel Smith (1996) agrees. "There are great bonds that run deep, even if we see each other once or twice a year. I call the Miss America family my second family."

Parting lessons

Achieving success for our Miss Americas after their reign ends is no accident. They know that having a tangible plan of specific goals and action steps comprise the ingredients of their recipes for achievement. Research has shown that the process of creating written goals is one of the most powerful life tools known and is a common denominator of high achievers.

When you make your goals concrete by writing them down, you set forces in motion to achieve them. Angie Baraquio (2001) came to understand the power of written goals during her years of competition. She had competed for Miss Hawaii over several years. But it wasn't until she wrote down her goal to become Miss America that she was able to harness her own commitment and discipline.

"I always go back to the quote, 'a dream is a goal with deadlines,' " said Angie. "To me that embodies the definition of a dream. Anything is possible. When I won Miss Hawaii, the Pageant sent me to a life-changing workshop called *What Matters Most*. In the workshop they told us to have short- and long-term goals. Here I was, twenty-four years old on the brink of a whole new life. I wasn't just Miss Hawaii. I could become Miss America. So I wrote down my goals. Number one was to be Miss America; number two was to get my master's degree and number three was to marry my high school sweetheart.

"I had several other goals, but those were my three most pressing ones. The odds of my winning were small. How many women out there want to become Miss America? Twelve thousand girls competed the year I won. It was such an amazing experience when I finally saw my face and signature as Miss America 2001 on the cover of the program book the following year.

"Writing down your goals so you can let them up to the universe is very powerful. You are then accountable to yourself. I ended up accomplishing all three of my most important goals."

Goals must be aligned with your purpose. Those people who don't want to be spectators to their own life and who want to shape its direction and outcome write their own story with their goal as the main story line. Then they write the subplots that will lead them to their happy ending. Once you know the what and why, you can figure out almost any how.

How do you actually write this plan that will be your guidebook? The task seems formidable. When you came up with your dream, you thought big. Now it's time to think small. If you are standing at the base of a mountain and look straight up, you think that you will never reach the top. By making sure you are physically fit, have the proper equipment, understand the best route and get the weather report, you can quiet your misgivings. Big goals are like that. By taking small steps now, pretty soon you'll be stepping out at the top of the sky.

Angie said, "The hardest part is having a goal. Once you make that decision you do an action plan, find little ways to reach it; baby steps make progress towards that goal."

Vonda Van Dyke (1965) believes you have to decide on your path, follow it and measure your progress. "I like to set small goals and have benchmarks for myself. Benchmarks are important because you know when you've accomplished something. It spurs you on to accomplish more."

Having specific goals gives you an advantage in decision making. When confronted with an important decision, your goals will provide the guidance to push you closer to your vision. You ask yourself if what you are doing right now will help you get where you want to go. If the answer is yes, then go for it. If no, make another choice.

Sometimes when we strive for success, we start to drown in the details. We're overwhelmed by what feels like an insurmountable heap of stuff. Remember the big picture and you'll find your head above water again.

Though it seems obvious, no perfect moment to start exists. Everything doesn't have to be in place or worked out in advance. That first baby step is the single most important action you can take to increase your chances of success.

Supercharge your goals

Most people get frustrated with their goals when they are unrealistic or non-specific with no way to evaluate progress or when stuff happens that throws them off course. Several simple steps can supercharge your goals and make them achievable.

The more specific your goal is, the more you give your brain information to figure out how to make it happen. Goals that are realistic and have a deadline and a measurable outcome set your gears in motion. It isn't enough to say you want to lose weight. Your specific goal might read to lose ten pounds in two months. Then when you set your action steps in place – working out three times a week for an hour and cutting out that mid-afternoon frappaccino – you've got your to-do list. When you achieve your identified outcome you can pat yourself on the back for a job well done.

Shawntel Smith (1996) counsels others who are striving to achieve their dreams. "The first thing is to make sure that the dream or goal you want to achieve is right for you. I would encourage you to dissect it and figure out what you need to do to make it a reality. You can't just wander aimlessly. You need a game plan and to know what step one, step two and step three are. As you accomplish things, check off those actions so that you can visually see yourself moving towards the goal you set before you.

"When I became Miss Oklahoma and when I was preparing to become Miss America, I had notebooks. In my interview notebook I had different issues listed. As I formed my ideas I would check them off. That helped me visualize myself getting closer to the end result."

Now that you have defined your goals, shored up your resolve and taken that first step, you have to decide what feats of daring you will commit to get to your dream. Some of them may be as mundane as clearing a pile of papers so that you can focus your brain, or putting together a budget of what you will need to fund your course. Other actions may require a major shift in thinking, like believing in the feasibility of what you once thought impossible and doing what you fear most.

Planning is not something you do once and then forget about. Planning must become part of your everyday life. Without a good plan and execution, you have little hope of achieving your goal. It can be as simple as every morning or the evening before writing your to-do list for the day and prioritizing those activities that will help you reach your goal the fastest. No rocket science here.

Plans are not static. Most bump up against the normal chaos of living. Those who rigidly adhere to their plan without any flexibility are doomed to fail. As you set your plan in motion, you have to be able to make adjustments as circumstances warrant. You need to plan the way a fire department plans. The fire chief can't anticipate fires, so he has to shape a flexible organization that is capable of responding to unpredictable events. He worries about the worst that can happen and develops plans to manage those worst-case scenarios. Most of the time those dreaded possibilities don't occur, so it is easier to deal with anything else that occurs. When something does, his team is prepared.

You've written your goals, set up your action plan, identified the resources you need, the obstacles that may slow down your progress and what to do about them. You think about the major and minor things that can inhibit your forward movement. What's the worst that can happen as you implement your plan? Once you have identified those worst-case scenarios, you can figure out how to minimize the impact of those events or where the opportunity lies within a potential catastrophe. The best time to explore alternative strategies is when life is calm and your head is clear.

Rebecca King (1974) counsels people who have a dream or a goal and don't quite know how to go about it to "never lose sight of it. If that's really where you want to be then you've got to research it. It may take you many paths to get there. Not everyone gets to that goal in the same way."

Tara Holland (1997) sums up how you can get the most out of life. "Decide what your dream is. A lot of time people have passions that they enjoy that they never really decide to pursue. You have to look at what your natural talents are, where your interests lie and decide what you want to do with that dream.

"Secondly, very importantly, is to determine your plan of action. How are you going to achieve that? That's where you write down a specific goal. I need to do x-y-z by January fifteenth to get where I want to be, whether it's training for a marathon, writing a book, getting a different job or getting a degree. If there is something that I just dread doing or it seems too big, I break it down.

"Thirdly, don't give up. I had peers who told me, 'You won't ever be Miss America.' I would look at them and say, 'Who are you to tell me I can't be Miss America?' They would say, 'I know you. You're no better than me. You're just an average kid, going to public school, doing normal things.' I said, 'You're right, I'm not any better than you, but I just may be more stubborn.' So it takes that persistence and stubbornness to follow through with your goals and your dreams.

"Fourthly, do what you say you will do. When we do what we say we will do, we develop confidence by discipline. You have to be organized about how you approach it. Decide your dreams, write down your plans and don't give up. Be persistent in sticking to those goals, modify when necessary. Create a short-term goal list of what you have to do to meet specific criteria in order to get to the next big step. Just lay it all out."

The journey is the joy

Ericka Dunlap (2004) said, "I feel like success is defined more by the journey in itself. You can really figure out what your success is based on how well you traveled your path. That's all there is to it."

When we dance, the objective is not to circle the room six times or end up in front of the punch bowl when the band hits its final note. Are you ever more in the moment than when you are moving to music? Your journey towards your dream should be savored the same way. You do have a destination, but it is in the doing that soul satisfaction becomes your dance partner.

The pathway to your dreams is never straight. The landscape will vary from lush mountains to barren deserts, but as long as you are traveling, new vistas keep opening up and new opportunities appear around the next bend. The journey is not just about achieving a specific end but being the best you can be on that journey. There is much satisfaction in that alone, regardless of the outcome. Who knows what other wonderful things might happen along the way?

Heather French (2000) gains knowledge with every step and counsels others to do the same. "I encourage young women that whatever road they are traveling, they need to be aware of all the lessons that are available on that road. Nothing is a final destination. A lot of people see Miss America as *the* final destination. But most of us when we get there realize that it is another stepping stone to something else. It has allowed us to climb a ladder a little higher to see what else we can do. We will be the last to tell you that we are doing enough. When I get together with my Miss America sisters, we talk about how we need to be doing more. Our perception of doing more is perceived by a lot of others as ludicrous, that it's not even attainable. But we did it once. We can do it again."

Susan Powell's (1981) definition of success has changed, just as it has for so many Formers. "Success is finding a passion in your life that gives your life meaning. Over the years my definition has become richer because it is much more internal than ever before. It's been primarily about my music and being able to make a living doing that. In my twenties it was a lot about beating myself up that I wasn't working hard enough. Now in my late forties, the edges are much smoother. You start to see the big picture. My relationships are much more of a priority for me, mixed with my passion for music. I've gotten a lot better at a lot of things. I'm an artist. I love to cook and have people over for dinner. I love to play cards and I love to laugh. My life is richer now because I now have all those things every day in my life that I didn't allow myself to really love when I was in my twenties."

The journey to wherever you are going is the experience of really being alive. There is a big difference between planning for the future and living in it. If you were told that you would die in a year, I would bet that what you want are experiences, not material things and not money

– except enough to fulfill your desires. People who go through traumatic events find that their priorities change. What have you always wanted to do? Answering that question will help you find your joy.

Showing up is 90 percent

Our Miss Americas learned early on that they had to be present to win, not only the crown, but at every endeavor they ever pursued. Amazing stuff happens when you just show up. People sometimes say that others are lucky when something happens that moves them closer to their goals. But in fact those people who got lucky, showed up. They made sure that they were in a place where luck could happen to them. They had prepared themselves to be open and ready for luck. If you are not in the place where and when opportunities happen, no amount of luck will make a difference. No one got the job who didn't show up for the interview or the actor get the part who didn't show up for the audition. Even the rare person who wins big at the lottery showed up at the convenience store to buy a ticket and then later to collect her winnings.

Kylene Barker (1979) knew her success had little to do with luck. "It was late in the afternoon and I had just returned to my locker from gymnastics practice. I hear one girl whisper to another, 'Oh that Kylene, whatever she touches turns to gold. That's what you call being born under a lucky star.' Maybe I should have been flattered, but I wasn't. I was furious. Lucky star, my foot! Where was the whisperer all those freezing cold mornings when I would wake before dawn to practice for an upcoming gymnastics meet? Where was she when I was bandaging the countless skinned knees and soaking the painful pulled muscle? Where was she when I was psyching myself up, willing myself to win when I was frightened and doubtful of my abilities? What was she doing when I was making lists of my weaknesses and strengths and trying to develop the control to capitalize on my strengths? Forget about luck. Winning is a lot of things, but it is rarely blind luck."

Even though Rebecca King (1974) grew up in a farming town so small that it didn't have a stoplight, her vision for herself was as big as the world. She didn't accept that just because she came from limited means, she didn't have a broad array of opportunities open to her.

She worked to create her own luck. "I came from a little town of two hundred fifty people. My high school class of sixty-six was at a school in a town with a population of twenty-five hundred seven miles away. Even in a tiny farming community and a small-town high school, there are lessons to be learned.

"You have to take advantage of all the opportunities. Do something like putting on an event in the community to raise funds with the local Rotary so someone could go to band camp. It means stepping outside of who you are – as a twelve-year-old, as a fifteen-year-old and seeing a need and saying, 'I can help solve that.' It doesn't matter the size of the community. Then, because you may have been in the right place at the right time, new opportunities open up."

It's up to you

Don't take things for granted. Just because you've put your wishes out into the universe doesn't mean that they will come true all by themselves. Someone has to pay attention and that someone is you. Too many people have been lulled into a false sense of complacency when things are going their way. When the music stops and the lights grow dim, they wonder why no one is knocking on their door to sign them to a million-dollar contract. Follow in the footsteps of our Miss Americas, who never stop paying attention. They've already forged a trail.

Lee Meriwether (1955) is a great cheerleader when it comes to pursuing one's dreams. She knows that once is never enough. "Never, ever, ever give up. Never. Just keep at it in any way that you can. It doesn't always have to be the dream exactly as you first saw it. Maybe from another angle it changed, but underneath it's still the same dream. I would always look at it from every vantage point possible. The dream can change and still be true to its core. But boy, can it blossom, develop and flower. That's what's happened to me, like what I'm doing now. I never in a million years would have thought I would be doing children's theater. Right now I'm performing in a play as a wicked witch. The kids love it and I love doing it."

Being Miss America rewarded Lynda Meade (1960) with invaluable life lessons. "It taught me that if there is any goal, anything you want to do in life, just get on with it! For heavens sake, don't just sit around stewing about it, thinking about it. Jump in there and do it. That sounds so simple, but it's really hard for some people. They can't move. They're terrified. I don't know what you do with people who are that scared. You have to remember that wonderfully successful people can be quaking in their boots, just like you and me. That sounds trite, but it's true. When you have been thrust into a situation like being Miss America, you realize that everybody is thrust into some situation or another that is challenging. It's all about having goals and developing a plan, then doing it. It's that simple."

Your most important, though often least valued possessions, are your dreams. You future is a blank canvas waiting to be made into a masterpiece. It's up to you to pick up the paintbrush and choose the colors.

Our Miss Americas don't always know where life will lead them, but wherever they land, they work at making it a place they want to be. I hope you will take to heart the lessons our Miss Americas have shared.

- True beauty is forged on the inside.
- Success comes from following your heart.
- Have a compelling vision and share it.
- Emulate your highest ideal.
- Trust the universe to deliver – eventually.
- Be willing to embrace change.
- Be persistent, disciplined and committed.
- Believe in yourself.
- Forgive yourself often.
- Ask for help. People like to say yes.
- Remember that diamonds are made under pressure.
- Make your own luck.
- Invest in yourself, then others will too.
- Know that many paths lead to the same destination.
- Be specific in your intent and your goals.
- Keep your dream in front of you.
- And don't forget to show up.

Our Miss Americas have shared their intimate thoughts and the rich wisdom of their years through the lessons in *Pretty Smart*. In these lessons are all the tools you need to become your own Miss America and give your dreams the gift of flight. Now that's pretty smart!

Epilogue

"Well-behaved women seldom make history." Laurel Ulrich, Pulitzer Prize winning historian and Harvard University professor

Researching and writing *Pretty Smart: Lessons From Our Miss Americas* has been a most extraordinary journey for me. I've met warm and wonderful people I never would have met, learned about a world I knew little of, had adventures that I could not have imagined just a few short years ago and stretched myself in ways I didn't know I could bend.

Like lots of ideas, when I came up with the theme for *Pretty Smart*, I thought it was destined for the file cabinet. But after a while it took hold of me and wouldn't let go. So I poked at the concept for a couple of years to see whether it had legs. After that I had to decide if I would be willing to commit the time, energy, resources and angst I knew I would experience to bring it to life. It didn't take long for me to answer yes on all counts. Then I got serious. I had found my passion. Having never published a full-length book, this looked like one daunting task. I spent two and a half years powering my way through the researching, interviewing and writing of *Pretty Smart*.

My biggest regret in writing *Pretty Smart* is that, with reams of research and over eight hundred transcribed pages from more than thirty interviews with former Miss Americas, judges, Pageant coaches and former Miss Mississippis when I attended the fiftieth anniversary of the Miss Mississippi pageant, I had to make difficult choices about which stories to use. So much still sits in my files. When I flip through them, I come across story after story that is inspiring and insightful. I wish I could have included them all. Each of the fabulous and beautiful-from-the-inside-out women that I talked with was articulate and thoughtful in her response and a delight to get to know. I wish that each of you could have been there with me to experience their warmth and humanity in person.

In the process I learned so much about myself. I knew that to write about what it takes to find true success would mean that I would have to live out my own version of all the lessons taught by our Miss Americas. I struggled many times over with the very issues I've written about. I had to force myself to keep going when I was tired and overwhelmed, find the financial resources when money ran low, walk through my fear when rejection loomed and stick to my plan when distractions called. I'm proud of myself for having succeeded.

You would think that these universal lessons about what it takes to pursue your dreams would have yielded their wisdom to me years ago, but like the proverbial onion, each time I peeled away a layer, I discovered something new. I thought that passion would come in a flash, but I see now how it needs to be nurtured, tucked into a nest and kept warm. I found that my need for approval, fear of rejection and self-doubts still walk with me, but no longer have the power to control my actions that they did, once upon a time. Having stripped away so many false motivations, the language of my life is now so much more poetic.

As I talked to these remarkable women, I was impressed at how, at a very young age, they were already well into this dialogue with themselves about how they can achieve their goals and be their best. I think of myself in my twenties and thirties and how I cast about haphazardly as I tried to figure out all this for myself. But figure it out I did. Mostly. The process will never stop until I lie down to rest and never get up again. I know that if I ever felt stuck in the status quo, my life would be boring. The unexpected fires up my enthusiasm and energizes my efforts. I can't wait to find out what happens next.

My own definition of success has changed over the years. My ambitions for my career were satisfied in previous decades with high-level executive positions, the power to make change within an organization that came with those positions and the recognition attached to the title. Over the years I discovered what I considered to be worthwhile work that meshed with my values.

Now in the sixth decade of my life, I want to expand my repertoire of personal challenges met and joyful adventures experienced. I feel successful when I set goals, however small or large, and do whatever it takes to achieve them, whether it's weeding the garden or fertilizing my talent. For me, a big part of success is the journey of discovery that expands my horizons, tests my inner mettle and endows me with the wisdom to help others do the same.

It doesn't matter how old the calendar says I am, I feel like I'm just getting started and that the next decades will be the richest ever. That's the best lesson yet.

Acknowledgments

First and foremost, my deepest gratitude to the fabulous former Miss Americas who gave so graciously and generously of their time, insight, humor and thoughtfulness. Their very existence is what makes this book a possibility. They moved me with their stories, humility, courage and desire to make a difference: Jean Bartel, Lee Meriwether, Marilyn Van Derbur, Mary Ann Mobley, Lynda Mead, Donna Axum, Vonda Van Dyke, Phyllis George, Rebecca King, Tawny Godin, Kylene Barker, Susan Powell, Gretchen Carlson, Heather Whitestone, Shawntel Smith, Tara Holland, Nicole Johnson, Heather French, Angela Baraquio, Ericka Dunlap, Deidre Downs and Jennifer Berry.

A very special thank you goes to Phyllis George, Miss America 1971, for writing such an inspiring foreword, helping to shape the title, and whose encouragement and enthusiasm for *Pretty Smart* gave me wings; to Sam Haskell, Chairman of the Miss America Organization, for believing in the book from the minute I met him and for all the doors he opened for me. I couldn't have written this book without his warm and generous assistance. To Art McMaster, President and CEO, and Sharon Pearce, Director of Communications of the Miss America Organization, for their assistance in helping to make the launch of *Pretty Smart* so fabulous, as well as the national office staff, Liz Puro and Pat Gianni. To the former Miss Mississippis, Chalie Carroll Ray, Karen Hopson Hall and Allison Wells, who shared insights gleaned from their participation in the pageant system. Thank you as well to Leonard Horn and Vernon Desear who were judges at the Miss Mississippi pageant; Briggs and Pat Hopson, Jan Blackledge, Carol Campbell and the other folks at the Mississippi pageant who gave me such a warm Magnolia Magic welcome and made me feel like a VIP; and to Frank Deford and Bruce Jenner, both judges at the Miss America Pageant, and Justin Rudd, pageant coach, all of whom shared their insights about the women who participate and their perspective on what set the winners apart.

What-would-I-have-done-without-you special thanks to Prill Boyle, author of *Defying Gravity* and very dear friend, who was my most critical reader, teacher and ultimate midwife, telling me to push,

push as I neared the finish line. To Suzanne Sheridan, one of my key encouragers and photographer extraordinaire, who helped me format the pictures in *Pretty Smart* and to my fabulous readers, Judy Glassman and my husband Bob Minicucci, for their discerning edits. To my copyeditor, Angela Foote, who kept pace with me and fine-tuned *Pretty Smart* to a fare-thee-well.

So many family and friends were the wind beneath my wings. They inspired me, supported me, loved me no matter what and were my biggest cheerleaders: my role model auntie, Anne Ausubel, for her unbounded encouragement and emeritus membership in our mutual admiration society; Beth, John and Robert Minicucci, my adored stepchildren, for their interest and sincerity; Helen Block, Rebecca Brooks, Rozanne Gates, Karen Harman and Lucy Hedrick, who sat on my shoulder encouraging me every step of the way. A special thanks to Jessica Bram for helping me hone my writing skills and for her honest and straightforward critiques.

To my excellent cousin Jesse Ausubel for the generous gift of his wonderful old farmhouse on Martha's Vineyard where I found the solitude to focus my creative energies.

To my adored son, Justin, for listening to my laments and for being my go-to guy for all kinds of how-to information as well as the great joy of my life. And to my most darling husband, Bob, whose unfailing support, wise counsel, love and willingness to don a bow tie and chauffeur me wherever I need to go has earned my forever adoration. A loving thanks to my parents, no longer with us, who endowed me with the strength and optimism to find my way in the world, no matter what.

And finally to all the people I met on this life-changing journey who encouraged me and confirmed for me the ongoing fascination that the American public has with America's royalty, Miss America.

My life has been changed, and for the better, by all of you. My heartfelt gratitude.